STANDARD LOAN

UNLESS RECALLED BY ANOTHER READER
THIS ITEM MAY BE BORROWED FOR

FOUR WEEKS

To renew, telephone:
01243 816089 (Bishop Otter)
01243 816099 (Bognor Regis)

-2. DEC. 1997

Longman Essential Psychology
Series editor: Andrew M. Colman

DEVELOPMENTAL PSYCHOLOGY

EDITED BY

Peter E. Bryant
and
Andrew M. Colman

LONGMAN
London and New York

Longman Group Limited
Longman House, Burnt Mill
Harlow, Essex CM20 2JE, England
and Associated Companies throughout the world.

*Published in the United States of America
by Longman Publishing, New York*

This edition first published 1995

ISBN 0 582 27805 8 PPR

British Library Cataloguing-in-Publication Data
A catalogue record for this book is available from the British Library.

Library of Congress Cataloging-in-Publication Data
A catalogue record for this book is available from the Library of Congress.

Typeset by 25 in 10/12pt Times
Printed and bound by Bookcraft (Bath) Ltd

CONTENTS

NOTES ON EDITORS AND CONTRIBUTORS

PETER E. BRYANT took his first degree in psychology at the University of Cambridge and then worked for his PhD at the Medical Research Council Social Psychiatry Research Unit at the Institue of Psychiarty in London. Immediately after his PhD (1994) he had a post-doctoral spell in Piaget's department at the University of Geneva. He went to work in the Department of Experimental Psychology at the University of Oxford in 1967 and is now the Watts Professor of Psychology there. He was elected a Fellow of the Royal Society in 1991. He has written books on cognitive development and on children's reading and has recently co-authored with Terezinha Nunes a book entitled *Children Doing Mathematics* (1995).

GEORGE BUTTERWORTH took his doctorate in psychology at the University of Oxford. He is Professor of Psychology at the University of Sussex. He has published many articles on development in infancy and is currently researching the origins of referential communication in babies. He has been editor of the *British Journal of Developmental Psychology* (1989–93) and chairman of the Scientific Affairs Board of the British Psychological Society (1992–95). He edited *Infancy and Epistemology* (1982).

JOHN C. CAVANAUGH is Professor and Chairperson of the Department of Individual and Family Studies at the University of Delaware. His research interests include cognitive ageing, self-evaluation of memory, and cognitive impairment. He is co-editor (with Jan Sinnott) of *Bridging Paradigms: Positive Development in Adulthood and Cognitive Aging* (1991) and author of *Adult Development and Aging* (2nd edn, 1993).

JOHN C. COLEMAN obtained his PhD from the University of London. He is also trained as a clinical psychologist. He is currently the Director of the Trust for the Study of Adolescence, an independent charity and research organization based in Brighton, England. He is the editor of the *Journal of Adolescence*. His most recent books are *The Nature of Adolescence* (2nd edn, 1990) and *Youth Policy in the 1990s* (1992).

ANDREW M. COLMAN is Reader in Psychology at the University of Leicester, having previously taught at Rhodes and Cape Town Universities in South Africa. He is the founder and former editor of the journal *Current Psychology* and Chief Examiner for the British Psychological Society's Qualifying Examination. His books include *Facts, Fallacies and Frauds in Psychology* (1987), *What is Psychology? The Inside Story* (2nd edn, 1988), and *Game Theory and its Applications in the Social and Biological Sciences* (2nd edn, 1995).

SARA MEADOWS is Senior Lecturer in Education in the School of Education at the University of Bristol. She is the editor of *Developing Thinking* (1983) and the author of *Understanding Child Development* (1986) and *The Child as Thinker* (1993), which is a 200,000 word version of her contribution to this volume. She is co-author (with Asher Cashdan) of *Helping Children Think and Learn* (1988).

PETER K. SMITH is Professor of Psychology at the University of Sheffield. He has researched extensively on the topic of children's play, and is currently working on ways of dealing with bullying in schools. He is the co-author (with Kevin Connolly) of *The Ecology of Preschool Behaviour* (1980), and (with Helen Cowie) of *Understanding Children's Development* (2nd edn, 1991). He is co-editor (with D. A. Thompson) of *Practical Approaches to Bullying* (1991).

SERIES EDITOR'S PREFACE

The *Longman Essential Psychology* series comprises twelve concise and inexpensive paperback volumes covering all of the major topics studied in undergraduate psychology degree courses. The series is intended chiefly for students of psychology and other subjects with psychology components, including medicine, nursing, sociology, social work, and education. Each volume contains five or six accessibly written chapters by acknowledged authorities in their fields, and each chapter includes a list of references and a small number of recommendations for further reading.

Most of the material was prepared originally for the Routledge *Companion Encyclopedia of Psychology* but with a view to later paperback subdivision — the contributors were asked to keep future textbook readers at the front of their minds. Additional material has been added for the paperback series: new co-editors have been recruited for nine of the volumes that deal with highly specialized topics, and each volume has a new introduction, a glossary of technical terms including a number of entries written specially for this edition, and a comprehensive new index.

I am grateful to my literary agents Sheila Watson and Amanda Little for clearing a path through difficult terrain towards the publication of this series, to Sarah Caro of Longman for her patient and efficient preparation of the series, to Brian Parkinson, David Stretch, and Susan Dye for useful advice and comments, and to Carolyn Preston for helping with the compilation of the glossaries.

ANDREW M. COLMAN

INTRODUCTION

Peter E. Bryant
University of Oxford, England

Andrew M. Colman
University of Leicester, England

Developmental psychologists are interested in changes in behaviour that come with age. They want to know how and also why people are different at different times of their lives in the ways that they behave, in their feelings, and in their relationships to other people.

Developmental changes of this sort are at their most striking during childhood. The differences, for instance, between a six-month-old infant, unable yet to walk or talk, and a lively, competent two-year-old are quite remarkable, and these differences repeat themselves in environments that are radically different from one another all over the world. This is one reason why most, though not all, developmental psychology is about childhood. Another reason is the potential practical value of the topic. When we find the truth about the nature of children's intellectual and social development, surely we will also have the answer to most of the serious problems of education.

Three questions dominate research in developmental psychology. The first main question might seem paradoxical, given what we have just said about developmental psychologists' assumptions. The question is whether there is any fundamental developmental change in behaviour at all. There is a pressing reason for this question to be asked, because over the last 20 years or so research has shown that babies are apparently born in possession of some basic mechanisms that underlie and control quite sophisticated behaviour. In chapter 1 of this volume George Butterworth gives a clear account of some of this ingenious and important work. It is apparent now that the mechanisms that are responsible for the perception (both visual and tactual) of shape, for the recognition and discrimination of faces and facial expressions, and even for the coordination of information about size and distance and about shape and orientation (the constancies), are intact and at work very soon after the child is born. It has been shown that young babies can discriminate numbers, and one recent experiment (Wynn, 1992) even goes so far as to make a convincing claim that babies less than six months old can add and subtract small numbers. On the social side, as Peter K. Smith's chapter 3 and also Butterworth's chapter 1 remind us, several psychologists have claimed that babies are quite skilled in maintaining complex interactions with their parents in particular. If so many skills are innate, do we really have to continue with the traditional developmental idea of fundamental changes happening to children's behaviour again and again and right through childhood? Is it not possible that these changes are at the surface, and that the basic mechanisms that govern our behaviour are innate?

There are two reasons at least for thinking that a great deal in behaviour is not innate. One is that the new work on infants' skills deals with only a very small part of human behaviour, and most of that at the perceptual end (see, for example, Granrud, 1993). There is nothing yet, for example, to show that the ability to make logical inferences or to reflect on the nature of language is innate, and there are good empirical grounds for thinking that these are abilities that take children many years to master. The second is that it is actually impossible for all important human skills to be innate, because many of these skills involve human inventions — inventions that are not universal and that have to be passed on from generation to generation. It took mankind many hundreds of thousands of years to invent the alphabet — an extraordinarily efficient way of representing the sounds of words in a written form — and it is still quite hard for children to learn how the alphabet works. It would be preposterous to suggest that the skill for mastering the alphabet is innate, and no one seriously does so. Much the same could be said for our decimal number system, for the various methods of measuring that are so important a part of human activity, for perspective drawing, and for many social institutions, to take just a few examples. The idea that the transmission of the understanding of these cultural inventions is a legitimate topic for developmental psychologists was originally produced by Lev Vygotsky, a Russian psychologist, whose work and theories are described in chapter 2 by Sara Meadows. Vygotsky's influence is still a strong one in the study of social and cognitive development. For a further discussion of this issue, see Rosser (1994).

So, the right answer to the first question is that some aspects of human behaviour do not develop, but that others do, and this brings us directly to the second main question of developmental psychology, which is: what in human behaviour actually does develop and when do the developmental changes happen?

The case for an ordered series of developmental steps in various aspects of human behaviour has been argued by most great figures in developmental psychology. Jean Piaget's theory is probably still the best known example. His ideas centred on logic. Children's intellectual and social behaviour is constrained by their logical abilities, he claimed, and these logical abilities change dramatically during childhood. Most of Piaget's empirical work was designed to show how radical these changes in logical ability are and therefore how little logic young children can use when they try to solve problems or to understand what is going on around them. For example, he tried to show that young children cannot make deductive inferences about quantity of the form A > B and B > C implies A > C, and that they do not understand that a set of objects stays the same in number if its perceptual appearance is altered (by being spread out or bunched together, for example) and only changes numerically if it is added to or subtracted from. These claims about young children's logical ineptness are all hotly disputed, as Meadows's chapter 2 tells us, but so are the counter-claims against Piaget's theory (Smith, 1993). The whole issue of logical development remains a live and extremely interesting one.

Another possibility is that children's "information processing capacities" change. Here the idea, to be found in chapter 2, is that they can handle more and more information as they grow older and that this enables them to solve increasingly sophisticated problems. This approach does not necessarily conflict with Piaget's, even though the two have often been pitted against each other: both kinds of development, logical and informational, could be true.

It is not at all surprising that children's social behaviour has also attracted the attention of people interested in the possibility of there being an orderly development in human behaviour. In infancy the existence of a set of entirely predictable stages is now indisputable (see Butterworth's and Smith's chapters 1 and 3). Imitation, interest in faces, smiling, fear of strangers, upset at separation from parents – these are all aspects of infants' behaviour that emerge at particular ages and in a particular order. Smith's chapter 3 shows that much later on in childhood there are also quite noticeable and systematic changes in children's behaviour – for example, in aggression and in patterns of friendship. There is even a strong possibility of orderly changes in social behaviour as late as adolescence. The onset of puberty, in particular, as John C. Coleman's chapter 4 shows, may have far-reaching effects on children's social preferences and on their social reactions. For more information on adolescence, see Kimmel and Weiner (1995).

Thus, the case for development is strong. We can say that there are systematic changes in the way children behave as they grow older and that these changes almost certainly reflect underlying changes in the basic mechanisms that control our behaviour. This assertion leads us to the third main question in developmental psychology, which is a causal one. The question takes this form: given the fact that a clear and orderly development in many aspects of behaviour does take place with age, what makes these changes happen?

All developmental theories make causal statements. Vygotsky's causal hypothesis stemmed from his interest in cultural inventions. This led him to insist on the importance of the transmission of information from generation to generation, and thus from skilled adults to less skilled children. Children become more competent intellectually because they learn skilled acts: at first they manage these acts only with the help of competent adults but later can perform them without any support from others. Vygotsky's term for this hypothetical sequence of events was "the zone of proximal development", and his main idea about it was that children gradually internalize the support that they received from the adult: eventually they provide their own support.

This causal hypothesis contrasts quite strongly with Piaget's, which paints a picture of the child working things out on his or her own. According to Piaget the main spur for intellectual development is conflict. The child finds that he or she has two contradictory opinions about the same thing, and realises that this means that something must be wrong. The child resolves the conflict by reformulating the underlying thought processes, which then leads to an appreciable intellectual advance.

Both of these causal hypotheses are very broad and unspecific. They were designed to provide the cause of developmental change in general, and that actually makes them very difficult to test (as Meadows points out in Piaget's case in chapter 2), because they do not make explicit predictions about specific developmental changes. It is not surprising that neither Vygotsky, nor Piaget, nor any of their followers have produced any good evidence for these causal ideas.

Even specific causal hypotheses are quite difficult to test. The most direct evidence is from intervention experiments, and the simple rationale of these is that, if factor A causes development X, then intervention in the form of increasing a group of children's experience with A should speed up the development X. But there are some hypotheses where this method is simply impossible. That is the case with hypotheses (examples are described in chapter 3) about the importance of a secure relationship between parent and child. You, the experimenter, cannot − thank goodness − decide that from now on 20 children should no longer have a good relationship with their mother and father. But intervention experiments have been tried as tests of theories about the causes of various specific intellectual changes, such as learning to read. In such cases (see Meadows's chapter 2) the results of experiments are particularly convincing when combined with correlational evidence. For example, giving children extra experience with phonological judgements about the constituent sounds in words does help them learn to read, and it has also been shown that there is a strong predictive relationship between their ability to make such phonological judgements before they begin to read and the progress that they make in learning to read many years later (Goswami & Bryant, 1990). These two results, combined, make a strong case for the casual idea that phonological skills are an important determinant of learning to read, and they also encourage the idea that specific causal hypotheses are a great deal easier to establish than general ones.

Specific causal hypotheses may be easier to test, but that does not mean that they are more likely to be right, and in fact the question of specificity takes us right back to the question of the nature of development. If we take the specific approach, then one factor or set of factors will determine children's logical thinking and their mathematical understanding, and a completely different set of factors will prompt the children's growing competence with reading. If that is the case, then development is not all of a piece, because there is no connection and no similarity in the way that different aspects of behaviour develop. We do not know yet, because we still have not tested many of these specific hypotheses fully enough.

The question – whether "development" is no more than a descriptive term – is raised even more sharply by work on old age, which is developmental in the sense that here too human behaviour changes in a fairly systematic fashion with age, but which may have nothing to do with the changes that take place in childhood. Some of these later changes (which are so clearly described in John C. Cavanaugh's chapter 5), such as the decline in memory, look like the mirror image of child development, but this may be just a coincidence. Shakespeare noticed it in his famous description of the seventh age as "second childishness and mere oblivion, / Sans teeth, sans eyes, sans taste, sans everything" (*As You Like It*, II. vii). See Stuart-Hamilton (1994) for a more extended discussion of the psychology of ageing.

At any rate, developmental work on adults and research on children share not just a common concern with change but also common methods, and it is now clear that most of the valuable advances in studying development have stemmed from the invention of new and more sophisticated ways of studying developmental changes and the reasons for these changes. The research reviewed in the following chapters tells us very clearly about the ingenuity and freshness of contemporary developmental research and about the consequent successes of this lively branch of psychology. Readers who wish to delve deeper into developmental psychology should note that, in addition to the publications mentioned in this introduction, there are helpful suggestions for further reading at the end of each of the chapters that follow.

REFERENCES

Goswami, U., & Bryant, P. (1990). *Phonological skills and learning to read*. Hove: Lawrence Erlbaum Associates.
Granrud, C. (ed.). (1994). *Visual perception and cognition in infancy*. Hillsdale, NJ: Lawrence Erlbaum Associates.

Kimmel, D. C., & Weiner, I. B. (1995). *Adolescence: A developtnental transition.* New York: Wiley.

Rosser, R. A. (1994). *Cognitive development: Psychological and biological perspectives*, Boston, MA: Allyn and Bacon.

Smith, L. (1993). *Necessary knowledge: Piagetian perspectives on constructivism.* Hove: Lawrence Erlbaum Associates.

Stuart-Hamilton, I. (1994). *The psychology of ageing: An introduction* (2nd edn). London: Jessica Kingsley.

Wynn, K. (1992). Addition and subtraction by human infants. *Nature, 358*(6389), 749–50.

INFANCY

George Butterworth
University of Sussex, England

History of infancy research	Auditory-visual coordination
Prenatal development	**Perception and the development**
The perceptual world of the	**of skilled action**
newborn: the senses	Origins of knowledge of
Vision	physical objects in human
Hearing	infancy
Smell and taste	Origins of knowledge about
Methods of studying	people in human infancy
perception in babies	**The acquisition of language**
Perception of complex object	**Further reading**
properties in early infancy	**References**

Infancy is the period of development between birth and the onset of language, which covers approximately the first 18 months of life. There have been important discoveries about prenatal development and a great deal more has become known about the psychological origins of speech and language. The rather convenient markers, between birth and the appearance of first words, nowadays set only minimal boundaries with earlier and later stages of childhood.

HISTORY OF INFANCY RESEARCH

Systematic study of infants began in the nineteenth century. One of the earliest scientific studies was by Charles Darwin, who kept a diary of the development of his infant son William during the year 1844. He noted the baby's innate capacity for emotional expression, observations which were especially influential in Darwin's work on *The Expression of the Emotions in Man and Animals* (1872) and on Sigmund Freud in his theories of personality formation. Another particularly influential contribution was made by the German physiologist Wilhelm Preyer, who published a monograph *The Mind of the Child* (1895) based on observations of his own daughter from birth to $2\frac{1}{2}$ years.

The view of infancy that prevailed in the nineteenth century was most memorably captured by the philosopher and psychologist, William James, who described the world of the newborn baby as a "blooming, buzzing confusion, where the infant is seized by eyes, ears, nose and entrails all once" (James, 1890). This vivid phrase conveys an image of a passive infant, inundated by meaningless sensations, with little coherent awareness of self or of the outside world. The newborn was thought to have no more than reflex control of action and to be capable of seeing or hearing very little. One of the major scientific achievements since the mid-1960s has been radically to revise this nineteenth-century preconception in favour of an image of the infant as "competent" and well adapted to the demands of the physical and social environment.

By the early twentieth century, studies of babies had moved from single-case diary records to large-scale investigations. Two major schools of psychology soon emerged which generated rather dichotomous approaches to infant development. The behaviourist school, especially through John Watson, emphasized the importance of early experience in development. Watson and Raynor (1920) showed that irrational fears could be learned in infancy through the principles of association by classical conditioning, first demonstrated by Pavlov. An alternative emphasis was on intrinsic processes of biological growth. Arnold Gesell, who made extensive investigations of motor development in babies, is most closely associated with the "nature" side of the "nature–nurture" dichotomy, because of his stress on maturation. Gesell considered that the infant's motor development, from gaining of early head control to crawling and walking, unfolded on a rather inevitable biological timetable of "motor milestones".

The modern era of infancy research was inaugurated by Jean Piaget (1896–1980). Piaget rejected a dichotomy between nature and nurture in favour of an account of development that combines biology and experience. Piaget's main interest was in the intellectual development of babies. He studied his own three children in great detail to produce his "sensori-motor theory" of infant development (Table 1). He argued that development begins with a limited number of innate reflex actions which are triggered by specific sensory experiences. For example, babies are born with the sucking reflex which serves their nutritional needs. Soon, however, the baby applies the reflex to other objects, in repetitive exploration (circular reaction) and thus learns something of the variety of shape, texture, and consistency of objects.

Other biologically based reflexes, such as looking, listening, or grasping

2

Table 1 Piaget's hierarchical theory of intellectual development in infancy

Stage I Reflexes
Age Birth to 6 weeks: e.g., sucking

Stage II Primary circular reactions
Age 6 weeks to 3 months: first acquired habits, e.g., thumb sucking

Stage III Secondary circular reactions
Age 3–9 months: goal-directed behaviour, e.g., visually guided reaching

Stage IV Coordinated secondary circular reactions
Age 9–12 months: differentiation of means and ends in intentional acts, e.g., searching for a hidden object

Stage V Tertiary circular reactions
Age 12–18 months: application of established means to new ends, e.g., baby climbs on stool to reach object hidden in cupboard

Stage VI Representation
Age 18 months: mental combinations of means and ends
Insightful discovery of new means through active experiment, e.g., baby pulls in object through playpen bars using a stick

Toddler has concepts of object, space, time, and causes

are also applied to a variety of objects in exploration of the world; the senses become inter-coordinated and actions become hierarchically organized in goal-directed sequences. Through acting on the world the baby acquires basic knowledge of cause and effect and of the properties of physical and social objects.

Piaget therefore avoided the pitfalls of dichotomizing nature and nurture; he recognized both the intrinsic biological processes of growth and the role of the infant's actions in the construction of knowledge. However, research has shown that Piaget may have underestimated the abilities of infants and this needs to be taken into account to give a contemporary overview. This information comes from studies of the prenatal origins of behaviour and from the contribution of infant perception to the development of knowledge.

PRENATAL DEVELOPMENT

Human gestation takes 40 weeks between conception and birth. The germinal stage lasts 2 weeks after conception and is primarily a period in which the fertilized egg undergoes repeated division into identical copies. It ends when the fertilized ovum has become implanted in the uterus. The formation of the basic structures of the human occurs in the embryonic stage, which lasts to the eighth week. There is rapid differentiation of the fertilized egg, with formation of limbs, fingers, toes, and major sensory organs. By 8 weeks, the embryo is about 1 inch long, limb buds have appeared, eyes and eyelids have

3

begun to form. The foetal stage from 8 weeks to birth coincides with major developments of the nervous system. The foetus rapidly takes on distinctively human characteristics so that by 12 weeks it is easily recognizable. By 16 weeks it is 6–7 inches long but it cannot survive outside the mother's body. By 23 weeks the foetus has a sleep–wake cycle synchronized with that of the mother. The foetus continues to develop for the normal gestational term of 40 weeks, although, like all biological phenomena, there is natural variation in the time of onset of birth.

The normal western baby at birth, around 40 weeks, weighs about 7 pounds and is about 21 inches long. The head, which has grown fastest in utero, is disproportionately larger than the body. Head and neck take up about 30 per cent of the total body volume by comparison to 15 per cent at 6 years and only 10 per cent in adults. It is worth remembering that the changing proportions of the body pose particular problems in gaining motor control in infancy.

Before the 1970s little was known about foetal behaviour before birth. Although pregnant women often note feeling foetal movements at about 16 weeks gestation, they are aware only of the most gross movements. In fact, depending on the measuring technique, up to 20,000 movements per day can be recorded in the foetus of less than 16 weeks gestational age. The advent of real-time ultra-sonic scanning in the 1970s has offered a safe means of imaging foetal movements in utero. Ultra high frequency sound (outside the audible range) is transmitted into the pregnant woman's abdomen. The echoes of the sound are picked up electronically and converted to a visual image which provides a view of the foetus as it moves.

De Vries, Visser, and Prechtl (1984) have described 15 distinctively different movement patterns in the 15-week foetus; these include foetal breathing movements, where the amniotic fluid is regularly inhaled and exhaled, stretching movements, turning movements, and slightly later thumb sucking. These well-coordinated movement patterns occur under the relatively weightless conditions of the foetal environment. Some, like the foetal breathing movements, seem related to similar action patterns in postnatal life, a phenomenon called *anticipation*, because the behaviours show organization that will be essential later in development.

After 24 weeks, finer degrees of movement control are observed, including expressive facial movements. Foetal activity resumes, in the increasingly cramped living quarters, and is now subject to sleep–wake cycles.

The first postural reflex, to be observed at 28 weeks, is the tonic neck reflex (TNR). This is a pattern of coordinated muscular activity in which the baby extends the arm and leg on the side to which the head is turned, while flexing the opposite arm and leg. This so-called "fencer posture" continues to the eighth postnatal month. The typical orientation of the head is thought to predict whether the baby will be right or left handed.

The general explanation of many of the foetus's spontaneous movement patterns is that they serve to exercise the developing system and aid the growing joints take their correct shape. Another possible function of prenatal activity is that it provides a high level of input to the developing ears, eyes and other sensory receptors. The cutaneous (skin), taste, and olfactory (smell) receptors and the vestibular and auditory systems are functional by 24 weeks gestation. The visual system is functional by the 26 weeks. Another possibility is that the continuous rotation and "crawling" movements of the young foetus may prevent adhesion to the uterine wall.

It is very likely that there is a continuous relationship between some foetal movement patterns and postnatal forms of behaviour. De Vries et al. (1984) describe a stretch and yawn pattern at 10 weeks foetal age which suggests continuity in the organization of yawning and stretching movements throughout life. Less obviously, there may also be continuity across loco-motor patterns. The crawling movements of the 6-month-old baby and the typical alternating walking movements of upright locomotion may be related to the so-called "stepping reflex", a cyclic stepping movement made by newborn babies when supported in an upright posture. The stepping movements may in turn be related to foetal movements which prevent adhesion to the uterine wall (Thelen, 1984).

Such observations on foetal behaviour have led to a re-evaluation of the status of the newborn. The radical shift in environment from prenatal to postnatal life, the extra weight of the body, especially the head, rapid growth and new possibilities for the control of action through vision may contribute to the general "helplessness" of the newborn. However, the period of intra-uterine life may have been rather effective in preparing the baby for independent existence, not only in terms of the repertoire of motor movements but also in some early perceptual abilities.

THE PERCEPTUAL WORLD OF THE NEWBORN: THE SENSES

The evidence suggests that all the basic sensory systems are functional from birth or before; even newborn babies will show preferences in vision, hearing, taste, and smell. They actively seek out to what they will attend and this implies that babies are not passively bombarded by sensory stimulation, as William James had assumed. We shall briefly review the sensory capacities of the newborn before turning to research on the information which the senses make accessible to the baby.

Vision

Relative to adult standards, vision in the newborn is very poor. The eyes have a fixed focal length because the lens does not accommodate properly until about 3 months. However, the fixed focal length of 21 centimetres coincides with the average distance of the mother's face from the baby when the infant is held at the breast. So, even though distant objects will be blurred, important social objects can be seen from birth. Newborns can discriminate between stationary black and white stripes one-eighth of an inch wide and a uniform grey surface. Moving the stripes to attract visual following movements actually yields much finer measures of visual discrimination. It is also known that newborns see in colour, probably trichromatically, as in normal (non-colour-blind) adults.

Stereoscopic binocular vision, which is particularly useful for depth perception, does not begin to develop until about 13 weeks. This seems partly to be a function of poor control over the convergence of the eyes (when we focus both eyes on the same object the eyes converge differentially according to the object's distance), partly a function of changes in the axes of alignment of the eyes in the early weeks of life, and partly a function of "tuning" the visual cortex of the brain so that the neural cells responsible for binocular vision receive the same information from both eyes. Extensive research indicates that binocular aspects of visual functioning depend on early visual experience during a "sensitive" period when the binocularly activated cells in the visual nervous system undergo fine tuning as a result of visual experience. There are important implications for the treatment of squint (strabismus). The effect of a squint is that binocular cells do not receive the same input from equivalent regions of the two eyes, so it is important to realign the squinting eye surgically if steroescopic vision is not to be adversely affected.

Newborn infant eye movements are very similar to those of adults. Successive shifts of visual fixation from object to object are known as saccades. Newborn infants follow moving objects by making a series of saccadic jumps whereas smooth tracking movements of the eyes develop at about two months. The scanning pattern is internally generated and not simply a reaction to incident visual stimulation. This is important because it again suggests that the newborn baby is well prepared to explore the visual environment. Newborns are particularly likely to pick out the external edges of visual objects, although they will shift their gaze to the interior of an object if it has internal movement. They do not simply search at random but scan for salient features of objects (for a review of infant vision see Atkinson & Braddick, 1989).

Hearing

The auditory system is functional from before birth (Rubel, 1985). The inner ear has reached its adult size by 20 weeks gestation. The middle ear, with its complex structure of bones and membranes which mediate hearing, is well formed by 37 weeks gestation, although it continues to change shape and size into adulthood. The external ear acquires its adult shape at 20 weeks gestation, but it continues to grow in size until the child is about 9 years of age.

It is becoming increasingly clear that infants are attentive to sounds from before birth. Since the middle ear of the foetus is filled with amniotic fluid, the conduction of sound is quite different in utero than postnatally. The most likely source of sound to be internally transmitted is the mother's speech, especially the patterning of sound onset and offset, at frequencies that are not masked by the internal noise of the mother's heart beat and blood circulation.

It has been shown that newborns can distinguish their mother's voice from the voice of another woman, which suggests that aspects of the mother's voice may become familiar to the child in utero (DeCasper & Fifer, 1980). Newborn babies generally prefer voices in the female range (average frequency 260 cycles per second) to the male range (on average one octave lower at 130 cycles per second). Adults and even children will adopt a higher pitched tone of voice when addressing babies, as if this is a particularly effective way of speech "getting through".

Smell and taste

Newborn babies show a similar aversion to a sour taste as do adults. They can also discriminate sweetness and show contented emotional expressions to sweet liquids (Steiner, 1979). Newborn babies show a similar range of expressions when presented with smells that are unpleasant (rotten eggs), or pleasant (a milky smell, honey, or chocolate). Neonates also recognize the smell of their own mother's breast milk within the first 6 days of life (Mac-Farlane, 1975).

Methods of studying perception in babies

The fact that babies show spontaneous visual preferences means that it is possible to study what the infant chooses to look at. The pioneer of this technique was Robert Fantz (1965), whose visual preference method has come to revolutionize our understanding of the perceptual world of the infant. The method is actually very simple. The infant is presented with a pair of visual targets, one to the left and the other to the right of the mid-line. The investigator notes the direction of the baby's first eye movement and the total amount of time that the infant fixates the target. It was soon established that babies prefer to look at patterns rather than plain surfaces; in one study it was found that newborns showed a preference for a face-like stimulus. Research has confirmed that newborns do indeed have a particular interest in faces and face-like stimuli (Johnson & Morton, 1992).

A variation of the Fantz technique involves presenting babies with the same stimulus repeatedly. This is called the habituation method, since it involves accustoming the baby to the visual object so that the object becomes progressively less interesting. Then, once the infant's attention has declined, a new object is presented. If the baby can perceive the difference between the old stimulus and the new one, she will show a marked interest in the new object. Thus, even where there is no initial preference between two stimuli, this method creates the potential for discriminating between a familiar stimulus and a new one, once again revealing what the baby perceives. Furthermore, the method also implies that the baby remembers something of the stimulus, since the procedure relies on the test material becoming increasingly familiar. Many contemporary studies of infant perception use variations of the visual preference and habituation methods to study not only vision but also aspects of audition, such as phonological perception (Kuhl & Meltzoff, 1986).

Perception of complex object properties in early infancy

Two very important features of visual perception are size and shape constancy. Changes in distance or orientation of an object from the observer result in differences in the projection of the retinal image. Size constancy refers to perceiving the real size of an object, despite the fact that the size of the retinal image varies greatly with the distance of the object. Shape constancy is the ability to perceive an object's real shape, despite any changes in orientation with respect to the observer which will result in changes in the projected shape of the retinal image.

Piaget believed that babies have to learn to coordinate touch with vision in order to perceive size and shape constancy. He suggested that having learned to grasp the object, the baby could twist and turn it, bring it further and nearer in the field of view, and gradually make the discovery of size constancy. The assumption is that "touch tutors vision" in early development. Piaget suggested that the visual world of the newborn baby is two-dimensional and lacking in depth, and that perception of shape and size constancy develops only slowly, during the first 6 months of life. A radical alternative to this traditional view of visual perception was developed by James Gibson (1966), who argued that perception should be considered an active process of seeking after information, with no privileged relation of any one sense over any other. While each of the senses has specialized functions, such as visual perception of colour or cutaneous perception of temperature, there is also information common to different senses. According to Gibson, perceptual systems have evolved to put the infant in direct contact with the real world from the outset. Competent perception could be a particular advantage, since the infant is typically much less able to make motor responses than to perceive: she will spend many months looking and listening before motor development allows physical exploration of distant objects.

The first demonstration of size and shape constancy in 3-month-old babies was made by Bower (1966). His finding has since been replicated in newborns by Slater (1990). Many new findings about the relations between sensory systems in early perception have come to light. These studies present a novel

8

picture of the "competent" infant, well able to gain information about the world through perception.

Auditory-visual coordination

Wertheimer (1961) first showed that there is an innate coordination between seeing and hearing, such that when the newborn baby hears a sound, the eyes will be reoriented to the sound. These results have subsequently been extended by Castillo and Butterworth (1981), who showed that newborns look to a distinctive visual feature of the environment in order to locate the source of a sound. Vision and audition interact in sound localization from birth. This is not to say that these coordinations are fixed and unchanging. In fact, there is a complex development; the innate coordination lasts for the first 2 months and then eye movements to sound become increasingly difficult to elicit until 5 months, when the coordination reemerges. U-shaped functions are rather common in early development and imply developmental reorganization of perceptual systems to give rise to new abilities.

As mentioned earlier, infants recognize their mother's voice soon after birth and there is also evidence for an early olfactory preference for the mother. Bushnell, Sai, and Mullin (1989) found that 5-day-old babies preferred to look at their own mother rather than another woman. It is possible that an innate coordination between hearing and seeing helps babies rapidly discover what their mothers look like. Prenatal familiarity with the mother's voice, coupled with an innate tendency to look where a sound is heard, may be sufficient for the baby to learn rapidly the distinctive aspects of the mother's appearance. By 3 months there is definite evidence that babies know the characteristic faces and voices of both parents. In a study by Spelke and Owsley (1979) the baby heard a tape recording of the mother's voice over a loudspeaker placed exactly between the mother and father. Babies from 3 months looked towards the mother when the mother's voice was heard (and towards the father when the father's voice was played). This need not be a very precise auditory-visual memory but the infant is nevertheless familiar with the sound and sight of the parent and this has important implications for social and emotional development, as will be discussed below.

Other aspects of inter sensory perception in young babies have important implications for the acquisition of speech and language. Kuhn and Meltzoff (1982) showed that babies detect a correspondence between the auditory and visual information for vowel sounds. This ability to "lip read" might be very useful in acquiring language as it means that visual and auditory information for speech are to some extent overlapping. Meltzoff and Moore (1977) showed that newborn babies can imitate tongue protrusion, mouth opening, and lip-pursing movements. As in many other newborn behaviours, a U-shaped developmental function was found, with imitation of tongue and mouth movements dropping out at about 3 months and reappearing at 12 months. The later form of imitation has a symbolic quality, as illustrated by Piaget, who observed his daughter use tongue protrusion in an attempt to understand how the sliding drawer of a matchbox might work. This observation shows that foundational abilities observed in the neonate should not be confused with more developed forms of the same behaviours seen later in development.

PERCEPTION AND THE DEVELOPMENT OF SKILLED ACTION

Perception has a particularly important part to play in the acquisition of skills in infancy. A motor skill is an organized sequence of goal-directed activity which is guided or corrected by feedback. Among the most important developmental precursors of skills are gaining control over the posture of the head by about 3 months, over sitting by about 6 months, and over standing towards the end of the first year. Vision serves an important role in gaining postural control since visual feedback from the stationary environment can be used to stabilize involuntary swaying movements when learning to sit or stand. Acquiring control over head and trunk enables new skills to be acquired, such as reaching and grasping, which depend on postural stability. The onset of independent locomotion also depends on good prior control of static postures. Each skill has a prolonged period of development and it is not surprising that infants with visual impairments are also delayed in postural control and the onset of locomotion.

The neonate is not entirely devoid of coordinated actions, indeed in some domains, such as sucking, the baby soon acquires very skilled control over the pressure and vacuum produced by the mouth in obtaining milk. In other domains, such as reaching to grasp something or in acquiring independent locomotion, only the most basic elements of the visual-motor coordination can be observed and skilled control takes many months to be acquired.

There is now quite extensive evidence for an innate eye hand coordination. Bower (1982) demonstrated that newborns will attempt to make gross, visually elicited, movements of the hand and arm in the vicinity of an attractive object. The visual object elicits a rather ineffectively aimed "swipe" with occasional contact. As the baby's aim gets better, contacts become more frequent; by about 4 months, the baby succeeds in grasping the object after contacting it. The actions of visually elicited reaching and tactually elicited grasping become coordinated and reaching begins to be visually guided in the course of the action (rather than "pre-programmed", as before). The infant begins to "anticipate" the object and the hand begins to open before contact so that, by 5 months, both reaching and grasping are coming under visual control. Once the right and left hand reach and grasp under visual guidance, they begin to collaborate and the baby will transfer objects from right to left,

Table 2 Integration of vision, action and memory in development of reaching and grasping

Age	Action pattern
9–12 months	Bimanual collaboration Differentiated grips between left and right hands
6–8 months	Integration of action and visual memory Search for hidden objects Transfer of objects between hands Development of finger grips
5–6 months	Reach is continuously guided to target by vision Mainly palm grips
Innate	Reached aimed at target by vision

in order to deal with more than one object at a time. This marks the beginning of a further integration of visually guided reaching with memory.

Table 2 illustrates the hierarchy of processes involved in the development of reaching and grasping and the approximate ages at which each level of skill is achieved.

Table 3 Locomotor development

Months	Motor behaviour
1	Lifts chin when prone; holds head erect for a few seconds
2	Lifts head up when prone
3	Rolls from side to back
4	Lifts head and chest when prone; holds head erect continually
5	Rolls from side to side
6	Sits with slight support
7	Can roll from back to stomach, stepping reactions
8	Tries vigorously to crawl; sits alone for short time
9	Can turn around when left on floor; makes some progress crawling
10	Stands when held up
11	Pulls self up by furniture
12	Crawls on hands and knees; side steps around inside cot
13	Stands alone
14	Walks alone
15	Climbs stairs
16	Trots about well
17	Climbs on a low chair; stoops
18	Can walk backwards
19	Climbs stairs up and down
20	Jumps; runs

Source: After Griffiths, 1954

Developments in the grips of babies can be observed well into the second year of life, as the infant first becomes able to grasp objects and then to gain finer and finer control over the fingers. Babies first grasp by pressing all the fingers against the object in the palm of the hand. These palm grips give way to more precise finger grips so that, by the end of the first year, the baby is able to pick up rather small objects in a "pincer grip" between the end of the index finger and the tip of the thumb. This precision grip is species-specific to humans. It involves full opposition of the fingers and thumb, so that they may be brought into contact for very skilled tool use, as for example in sewing or writing.

These observations once again show that the amount of pre-adaptive structure available in early development is greater than traditional theories would suppose, yet the baby only slowly gains the skills required to put the innate eye–hand coordination to use. Many other motor skills also come under visual control during infancy. Table 3 shows month by month the motor development to be expected in the average child (Griffiths, 1954).

ORIGINS OF KNOWLEDGE OF PHYSICAL OBJECTS IN HUMAN INFANCY

As adults we know that when one object is occluded by another, the hidden object continues to exist and to retain its physical and spatial properties. Furthermore, the movements of the object and its transformations are subject to regular physical laws and are therefore predictable. This is known as the "object concept", a shorthand way of expressing the fact that objects are permanent, substantial, and possessed of constant shape, size, and identity.

According to Piaget, the object concept stands at the foundations of thought. He was of the opinion that, until the child is about 18 months old, appearances and disappearances are not understood as the movements of single objects in space. His evidence came from infants' failure to search manually for hidden objects before 9 months. Indeed, he argued that for the young baby the object is a "mere image", lacking permanence, substantiality, and identity (Piaget, 1954). Piaget's theory rests heavily on the assumption that perception is insufficient to inform the developing child about the physical world. According to Piaget, infants fail to search for a hidden object because they do not perceive that it continues to exist once it disappears. If Piaget's interpretation of search failures is correct, then the physical universe of the infant must be very different to that of the adult.

However, Piaget's theory of the origins of foundational concepts has come under increasing criticism. One source of evidence against Piaget's theory came from infants born without arms or legs following the thalidomide tragedy. These babies often showed normal intellectual development, despite the fact that they lacked the opportunity for extensive physical interaction with objects (DeCarie, 1969). Other evidence against the Piagetian theory came from ingenious experiments based on the possibility that the infant may be capable of picking up information through the distal senses, especially through vision. Renée Baillargeon (1987a, 1987b) has systematically measured infants' perception of physical objects using the habituation method described earlier. Her technique involves habituating the baby, then changing the visual display in such a way that a basic physical law is broken. Changes in looking patterns reveal which changes in physical events babies perceive as possible or impossible.

For example, Baillargeon's experiments on perception of substance violate the principle that a solid object cannot move through the space occupied by another object (Baillargeon, 1987b). Babies of $3\frac{1}{2}$ months observe a screen, in the form of a drawbridge seen end-on by the infant, rotate repeatedly in a 180-degree arc. Once the infant has become habituated to this display, a large box is placed behind the screen and the infant is shown one of two test events. In one event, the physically possible case, the screen stops rotating when it is obstructed by the box. In a second, impossible event, the screen continues to rotate through a full 180 degrees, as if the box were no longer behind it. Babies looked longer at the impossible event than at the possible event. This suggests that infants perceive the continued existence of the hidden box and that they also perceive that the screen could not rotate through it. In subsequent experiments, Baillargeon went on to demonstrate that, by $6\frac{1}{2}$ months, babies understand not only that the screen should stop when there is a box behind it, but also that the screen will stop at different positions depending on the height of the box, or depending on whether the object behind the screen can be compressed or not. That is, the baby appropriately perceives occlusion and the possible physical interactions between rigid and elastic objects, and finds it unusual when the experimenter presents the baby with visual events that violate basic physical laws.

This evidence suggests that infants are able to perceive that solid objects cannot travel through the space occupied by other solids and that objects cannot appear at two separate points in space without travelling the distance between them. The important question is *why* does it take babies 8 or 9 months before they will search for hidden objects? Why is there this disjunction between *perceiving* the physical properties of objects and *using* the information to retrieve them? Baillargeon suggests that the limitation lies in planning sequences of action. The baby perceives the world appropriately, but until 8 or 9 months of age, lacks the ability to transfer information obtained through perception to memory, in order to regulate action.

ORIGINS OF KNOWLEDGE ABOUT PEOPLE IN HUMAN INFANCY

Whereas Piaget was mainly concerned to explain intellectual development in infancy, John Bowlby (1907–1990) was concerned to understand emotional development. He developed a unique synthesis of method and theory drawn from the traditions of Freudian psychoanalysis, recording of natural history, field studies of ethology (the study of animal behaviour in the natural environment), and cognitive developmental psychology, to explain the formation of the earliest attachment bonds between infant and mother (Bowlby, 1971).

A key idea in Bowlby's theory is that the mother provides a secure base from which the developing infant can explore the world and periodically return in safety. The evolutionary function of such attachment behaviour is thought to be to protect the child from predators; the further implication is that emotionally secure bonds between parent and child have basic survival value. Parental responsiveness to the exploratory instincts of the child is an important factor in establishing a secure attachment relationship; this in turn leads into a range of psychologically healthy developmental pathways. Securely attached infants feel free to explore a novel environment, so long as the mother is within sight. Bowlby argued that insecure patterns of attachment contribute to the formation of a neurotic personality, and that enforced, prolonged separations from loved parent figures, especially when a parent dies, may result in the long-term developmental links in psychopathology, such as depression in adulthood.

An early, practical application of his ideas arose in the changes that he effected in the hospitalization of young children in Britain. As a result of his work on prolonged and non-understandable separation, mothers were allowed to remain in hospital with their young children. Subsequent elaborations of the work have included large-scale epidemiological studies which have explored the role of family experiences as antecedents of depression and anxiety disorders (see Campos, Barrett, Lamb, Goldsmith, & Stenberg, 1983, for a review of socio-emotional development in infancy).

THE ACQUISITION OF LANGUAGE

A popular way to explain the fact that humans typically acquire language is by recourse to an innate "language acquisition device" (Chomsky, 1980). On this view, language is the near-inevitable consequence of the infant living in a particular linguistic community. An alternative theory, rather more consistent with the evidence reviewed above, is that language development brings together a variety of constituent processes, some of which can be observed very early in infancy, while others emerge with cognitive development. Some of the constituent perceptual abilities are not species-specific to humans, as in the case of phoneme perception (Kuhl & Meltzoff, 1986), while other abilities, such as pointing, are species-typical and closely linked to the comprehension and eventual production of speech. Early pre-speech abilities include sound perception and its counterpart in the production of babbling. Social interaction skills — such as "turn taking" between infant and mother, the emotional attunement of the infant to the mother, and attending jointly to a brief account of three major theoretical paradigms and two important areas of cognitive activity. (For a more extensive account, see Meadows, 1993.)

SOME FUNDAMENTAL THEORETICAL ISSUES

A number of profoundly difficult theoretical questions underlie the study of cognitive development, and theorists' different assumptions about these questions surface in their answers (or in their unawareness that they need to be answered). One collection of questions has to do with the degree to which cognition is a coherent set of general skills, applicable to all sorts of problems and disciplines, available to all normally competent human beings as a permanent part of their repertory, independent of the knowledge they are applied to, and best described in abstract, formal terms, rather than an ad-hoc bundle of task-specific procedures, culturally constituted, heavily dependent on the knowledge base available, and re-created each time they have to be used. Beyond this are questions concerned with the nature of development: is it unidimensional, is it consistent over different areas, is it a gradual, steady, quantitative change, or a matter of more sudden, qualitative shifts? Is it a matter merely of change or one of progress and improvement? How far is development internally generated, and how far is it a matter of external shaping? More importantly still, how are externally given and internally generated cognitions combined? Is the developing cognitive person best described and best explained as an information-processing mechanism, as an adaptable organism, or as a participant in a social construction? How much does the child's cognition differ from the adult's? What are the causes of any cognitive differences (or indeed any similarities) – differences in brains? In the amount, the organization or the availability of information? In control and awareness? In processes? In practice and expertise? In social position and experience? Finally, there are a number of questions that are fundamental but outside the main body of work on cognitive development: what about individual differences in cognitive development? What internal and what external characteristics and events improve or worsen cognitive development? What are the developmental links between cognition and other psychological systems?

These are profound questions: the aim of this chapter is to begin to elucidate them.

MAJOR THEORETICAL APPROACHES TO COGNITIVE DEVELOPMENT

Much scientific work has grown from particular theoretical paradigms, as researchers sought to refine, extend, criticize, or refute some earlier piece of work. The major approaches to cognitive development stem from the work

objects and events with the mother – all lay the groundwork for communication through language (Butterworth & Grover, 1989; Harris, 1992). Motor development enables the infant to gain control over the articulatory and gestural systems, while cognitive development promotes their use in intentional communication, in gestures such as pointing and in speech. Babies comprehend single words at about 9 months, most babies produce single words at about the end of their first year. Subsequent development proceeds rapidly as babies build up a vocabulary with increasing speed and discover the names of objects. The first two-word combinations begin at around 18 months and thereafter the child acquires the rudiments of grammar. Infancy has come to an end: the walking, talking toddler is now relatively autonomous and ready for new knowledge.

FURTHER READING

Bower, T. G. R. (1982). *Development in infancy* (2nd edn). San Francisco, CA: Freeman.

Bremner, J. G. (1988). *Infancy*. Oxford: Basil Blackwell.

Butterworth, G. E. (Ed.) (1982). *Infancy and epistemology*. Brighton: Harvester.

Osofsky, J. D. (1987). *Handbook of infant development* (2nd edn). New York: Wiley.

Slater, A., & Bremner, G. (Eds) (1989). *Infant development*. Hove: Lawrence Erlbaum.

REFERENCES

Atkinson, J., & Braddick, O. L. (1989). Development of basic visual functions. In A. Slater & G. Bremner (Eds) *Infant development* (pp. 3–36). Hove: Lawrence Erlbaum.

Baillargeon, R. (1987a). Object permanence in $3\frac{1}{2}$ and $4\frac{1}{2}$ month old human infants. *Developmental Psychology*, 23, 655–664.

Baillargeon, R. (1987b). Young infants' reasoning about the physical and spatial properties of a hidden object. *Cognitive Development*, 2, 179–200.

Bower, T. G. R. (1966). The visual world of infants. *Scientific American*, 215(6), 80–92.

Bower, T. G. R. (1982). *Development in infancy* (2nd edn). San Francisco, CA: Freeman.

Bowlby, J. (1971). *Attachment*. Harmondsworth: Penguin.

Bushnell, I. W. R., Sai, F., & Mullin, J. T. (1989). Neonatal recognition of the mother's face. *British Journal of Developmental Psychology*, 7, 3–15.

Butterworth, G. E., & Grover, L. (1989). Joint visual attention, manual pointing and pre-verbal communication in human infancy. In M. Jeannerod (Ed.) *Attention and performance* (pp. 605–624). Hillsdale, NJ: Lawrence Erlbaum.

Campos, J. J., Barrett, K. C., Lamb, M. E., Goldsmith, H. H., & Stenberg, C. (1983). Socioemotional development. In M. M. Haith & J. J. Campos (Eds) *Handbook of child psychology* (vol. 2, pp. 783–916). New York: Wiley.

Castillo, M., & Butterworth, G. E. (1981). Neonatal localisation of a sound in visual space. *Perception*, 10, 331–338.

Chomsky, N. (1980). *Rules and representation*. New York: Columbia University Press.

Darwin, C. (1872). *The expression of the emotions in man and animals*. London: John Murray.

DeCarie, T. G. (1969). A study of the mental and emotional development of the thalidomide child. In B. M. Foss (Ed.) *Determinants of infant behaviour* (vol. IV, pp. 167–187). London: Methuen.

DeCasper, A. J., & Fifer, W. (1980). Of human bonding: newborns prefer their mothers' voices. *Science, 208*, 1174–1176.

DeVries, J. I. P., Visser, G. H. A., & Prechtl, H. F. R. (1984). Fetal motility in the first half of pregnancy. In H. F. R. Prechtl (Ed.) *Continuity of neural function from prenatal to postnatal life* (pp. 46–64). London: Spastics International Medical.

Fantz, R. L. (1965). Visual perception from birth as shown by pattern selectivity. *Annals of the New York Academy of Sciences, 118*, 793–814.

Gibson, J. J. (1966). *The senses considered as perceptual systems*. Boston, MA: Houghton Mifflin.

Griffith, R. (1954). *The abilities of babies*. London: London University Press.

Harris, M. (1992). *Language experience and early language development*. Hove: Lawrence Erlbaum.

James, W. (1890). *The principles of psychology*. New York: Holt.

Johnson, M., & Morton, J. (1992). *Biology and cognitive development*. Oxford: Basil Blackwell.

Kuhl, P., & Meltzoff, A. N. (1982). The bimodal perception of speech in infancy. *Science, 218*, 1138–1141.

Kuhl, P., & Meltzoff, A. N. (1986). The intermodal representation of speech in infants. *Infant Behaviour and Development, 7*, 361–381.

MacFarlane, A. (1975). Olfaction in the development of social preferences in the human neonate. In Ciba Foundation Symposium 33 (New Series), Parent–Infant Interaction (pp. 103–117) Amsterdam: Elsevier.

Meltzoff, A. N., & Moore, M. K. (1977). Imitation of facial and manual gestures by human neonates. *Science, 198*, 75–78.

Piaget, J. (1954). *The construction of reality in the child*. New York: Basic Books.

Preyer, W. (1895). *The mind of the child*. New York: Appleton.

Rubel, E. W. (1985). Auditory system development. In G. Gottlieb & N. A. Krasnegor (Eds) *Measurement of audition and vision in the first year of postnatal life* (pp. 53–90). Norwood, NJ: Ablex.

Slater, A. (1990). Visual memory and perception in early infancy. In A. Slater & G. Bremner (Eds) *Infant development* (pp. 43–71). Hove: Lawrence Erlbaum.

Spelke, E., & Owsley, C. J. (1979). Intermodal exploration and knowledge in infancy. *Infant Behaviour and Development, 2*, 13–24.

Steiner, J. (1979). Human facial expression in response to taste and smell stimulation. In H. Reese & L. P. Lipsitt (Eds) *Advances in child development and behaviour*, (vol. 13, pp. 257–295).

Thelen, E. (1984). Learning to walk: Ecological demands and phylogenetic constraints. In L. P. Lipsitt (Ed.) *Advances in infancy research* (vol. 3, pp. 213–257). Norwood, NJ: Ablex.

Watson, J. B. & Raynor, R. (1920). Conditioned emotional reactions. *Journal of Experimental Psychology, 3*, 1–130.

Wertheimer, M. (1961). Psychomotor coordination of auditory and visual space at birth. *Science, 134*, 1692.

2

COGNITIVE DEVELOPMENT

Sara Meadows
University of Bristol, England

Some fundamental theoretical issues	Memory development
	Becoming literate
Major theoretical approaches to cognitive development	**Domains of cognitive development**
Piagetian theory	
Information-processing models	**Sources of individual differences in cognitive development**
Vygotskian theory	**Further reading**
Theories and issues in the development of cognitive skills	**References**

Studying cognitive development, we are concerned with "the child as thinker", with someone who thinks, understands, learns, remembers, and so forth. These are activities that are not completely understood even in their adult forms; accounting for cognitive development requires not only an understanding of the adult form but also of how it is reached, that is, we need to note what changes there are in cognition between different ages and to explain how these changes come about. An enormous amount of research and theorizing has been produced in an attempt to describe and explain the course of cognitive development. The disciplines relevant to a full understanding range from developmental neuroscience through computer science to cultural anthropology: each of these addresses a slightly different range of questions and has its own methodologies and theories. Because of the volume and heterogeneity of relevant work, it is not possible to produce a comprehensive synthesis: this review focuses on some of the fundamental questions in the field and on some of the recent developments, addressing them through

of Piaget, from the information-processing theorists of cognitive science, and from Vygotsky. Each deserves a brief review.

Piagetian theory

Piaget's theory of the development of cognition (Meadows, 1986, 1993; Piaget, 1983) has at its centre the child actively trying to make sense of the world, just as any organism must actively adapt to its environment. This cognitive activity is a special case of the adaptive processes that pervade all biological existence and evolution, "assimilation" and "accommodation". "Assimilation" is the relating of new information to pre-existing structures of understanding, and "accommodation" is the development of old structures into new ones at the behest of new external information or problems. These two together give rise to a series of structures of cognition, that is, to organized systems or "stages" of rules, categories, procedures, and so forth, which eventually amount to complex, comprehensive, coherent, flexible, and logically rigorous ways of understanding the world.

These stages are universal in that they can be applied to any cognitive problem, in that they operate at a consistent level across problems at any given moment, and in that all normal human beings develop them in the same order and at much the same rate, irrespective of cultural and educational differences, becoming increasingly logical, abstract, systematic, and flexible in their cognition as they move from infancy to adolescence. This cognitive improvement is caused by four interacting processes. These are organic growth, particularly the maturation of the central nervous system; the individual's experience of the actions performed on objects, both direct physical experience and indirect reflective experience of logico-mathematical rules and relations; social interaction, especially peer conflict rather than adult–child transmission of knowledge; and "equilibration", the most important and also the most problematic of the four.

Cognitive equilibration involves the idea that the organism needs to maintain a stable internal equilibrium within the changes and uncertainties of the outside world, and so automatically adjusts to the "perturbations" or "conflicts" which new or contradictory ideas or events produce in the cognitive system with just enough adjustment to get back to the original stable state or to get on to a new and better one where cognition finds a new more stable equilibrium. There are several conceptual roots of "equilibration majorante": in biologically programmed homeostatic mechanisms like those that stabilize the body temperature of warm-blooded animals; in the coherence, clarity, and consistency of logico-mathematical systems, in which no conflict or ambiguity is possible if the rules are properly applied; and in a belief that evolutionary adaptation involved a good and improving fit between the organism and the environment, and an unceasing progress towards better and better forms.

Piaget's is a rich and complex model that has made an immense contribution to developmental psychology, not least because it single-handedly put cognitive development at the top of the agenda, and also because Piaget sought to combine detailed observation of children's behaviour with the most profound questions about the nature of development, using ideas and evidence from biology, sociology, psychology, logic, and mathematics. It still has fervent adherents (Beilin, 1992). Nevertheless, it faces some significant difficulties Its abstract developmental processes – assimilation, accommodation, and (especially) equilibration – are hard to pin down conceptually or to observe or measure. Diagnosis of children's thinking has turned out to be problematic: their answers to questions seem to be somewhat unpredictably dependent on details of the questions and materials used (e.g., Donaldson, 1978; Light, 1986; Siegal, 1991); much post-Piagetian research has revealed surprising competence at considerably earlier ages than Piaget found. There is very little evidence for universal stages with consistent performance levels on all the tasks presumed to involve the same cognitive structure, and the more universal sequences found may be in a logically necessary order rather than a psychological one (Smedslund, 1980).

Piagetian theory emphasizes the individual child as the virtually independent constructor of his or her own development, an emphasis that undervalues the contribution of other people to cognitive development and excludes teaching and cultural influences. It seems possible that cognition is not so pure and abstract as Piagetian theory proposed, but may be rather more closely tied to particular tasks and routines, socially prescribed (Hinde, Perret-Clermont, & Stevenson-Hinde, 1985).

Information-processing models

Work in the "information-processing" tradition emphasizes precise analysis of how information is recognized, coded, stored, and retrieved in order to solve cognitive tasks, usually of a well-defined and tightly structured sort such as chess, balance-scale problems, or "Cannibals and Missionaries" (McShane, 1991) Researchers use the techniques of experimental cognitive psychology and computer science, and the central metaphor is that "people are in essence limited capacity manipulators of symbols" (Siegler, 1983, p. 129). Thus cognition involves the use of a fairly small number of basic cognitive processes in a structured way over a period of time, the same basic processes for all problems, though in different combinations and sequences. Cognitive development may involve development of basic processes, of the information base they are applied to, of the structure of the sequence in which basic processes are used, of the executive control of the whole system, or of combinations of these.

"Basic processes", such as recognition, categorization, association, coordinating different modalities and different information, appear in a rudimentary form even in the very youngest children (e.g., Butterworth, 1994; Harris, 1983; Kail, 1991), but undergo experience-related and age-related changes in speed, exhaustiveness, and flexibility. Learning and development use cognitive processes which are quite complex even from infancy; development here is a matter of refining cognitive tools rather than of creating them. It seems unlikely that cognitive development during child-hood involves the appearance of completely new basic processes, though the processes inherited from infancy may well change. The information base that cognitive processes are applied to, on the other hand, clearly increases enormously during development. This is so obvious that many theorists have set it aside as uninteresting or even a contaminating variable, but later researchers suggested that the amount, organization, and availability of information may have important effects even on universal cognitive processes (Chi & Ceci, 1987; Keil, 1989).

The structured use of basic cognitive processes and executive control of processing are seen as major areas for developmental improvement, as dis-cussion of memory and reading later in this chapter will describe: it seems clear that young children less often show deliberate strategic approaches to problems and have smaller and less flexible repertoires of strategies than older ones. This improvement, though age-related, may be connected with practice and the growth of expertise rather than with age per se.

There are various different information-processing accounts of how development comes about (Meadows, 1993; Sternberg, 1984) using similar ideas. Events that co-occur are associated; procedures that run many times become automatized; consistencies and inconsistencies are detected and sorted out. Earlier information-processing accounts, using serial processing as a model, emphasized executive control and monitoring: although there has only been a limited degree of success in producing a program that can act as a general problem solver, this approach has had some impressive results in modelling sequential logical problem solving in areas such as chess or the computation of whether a beam will balance. The development of Parallel Distributed Processing (PDP) or Connectionism promises progress with some of the cognitive areas that are less logical and sequential, such as the structure and acquisition of concepts (McClelland et al., 1986).

The basic hypothesis of PDP is that information processing involves a large number of units working contemporaneously in parallel, with units, like the neurons of the brain, exciting or inhibiting one another. Units that are active together have their excitatory connections strengthened and their inhibitory connections weakened; for units that are not active together inhib-itory connections are strengthened and excitatory ones weakened. Thus over time a network that repeatedly receives the same input will develop high-strength connections so that units that have repeatedly been active together will come to excite one another more reliably and strongly than ever. Units act on small items of information ("subsymbols") and the whole network will

21

come into play even if only some of the units are activated; no one sub-symbol is crucial and even the inclusion of a few incorrect or irrelevant ones will not throw the network if the general pattern of activation is correct. Networks can deal with possibilities and probabilities, rather than requiring complete and completely correct and non-redundant information as more traditional models do.

Connectionist models look closer to the biological structure of the brain, and their performance may be closer to the cognition of human beings on tasks such as pattern recognition in reading or the identification of what category a complex case belongs to (Clark, 1989). They look promising as models of the change that occurs during development or learning, and also of the effects of damage to a cognitive system. They will at least supplement traditional information-processing accounts of sequential problem solving with models of how problem solutions are learned and of how processing that is less linear is dealt with, and they may supersede them.

Vygotskian theory

Both Piagetian theory and the information-processing approach assume that there are psychological structures in people's minds that explain their behaviour, which are invariant across cultures, settings, and tasks, and which are essentially independent of the individual's relations to other individuals, to social practices, and to the cultural environment. Cognitive development is the individual construction of an internal mental model of external reality. Vygotskyian theory (Kozulin, 1990; Meadows, 1993; Tharp & Gallimore, 1988; Vygotsky, 1978, 1986) challenges this assumption; cognitive abilities are not internal and individualistic, but formed and built up in interaction with the social environment, interpsychological before they become internalized and intra-psychological. Children develop sophisticated cognitive competences despite starting with only rudimentary ones because adults are available as teachers or models to guide the child repeatedly through the relevant behaviour. The more expert person provides a context or "scaffolding" within which the child can act as though he or she was competent to solve the problem, and by so acting in such a context the child can indeed reach the solution successfully.

As the task becomes more familiar and more of it is within the child's competence, the adult can leave more and more for the child to do until at last he or she can undertake the whole task successfully. The child undergoes an apprenticeship in the skills of the culture, and by practising these skills and reflecting on them internalizes the cognitive tools that earlier members of the culture have developed. The developing thinker does not have to create cognition out of an unpeopled vacuum, but will first imitate and then internalize sole of the cognitive content and processes provided by others, and may in turn develop and pass on these skills. The internalized cognitive skills remain social, both in the sense that as mature learners we may "scaffold" ourselves through difficult tasks in an internal dialogue about our performance as our teachers once scaffolded our earlier attempts, and in the sense that for most individuals the only cognitive skills practised to a high level of competence are those that their culture offers; thus cognitive potential may be universal but cognitive expertise is culturally determined. Culturally given ways of thinking, remembering, categorizing, reading, and so forth build on and may supersede the biologically based ways we begin with.

As so much social interaction, and especially so much teaching, involves language, the Vygotskian model sees language development and cognitive development as becoming interrelated (Kozulin, 1990; Vygotsky, 1986). Children under about 2 years use vocal activity as a means of social contact and emotional expression, and are capable of systematic and goal-directed activity that does not require verbal operations. This first stage of "pre-intellectual speech" and "pre-verbal thought" is followed by a stage of "practical intelligence" in which there are parallels between the syntactic and logical forms of the child's language and the child's practical problem solving activity but no systematic or mutually useful links between them. Later, children start to use symbols external to themselves, such as language or other cultural tools, to help with their internal problem solving; at this stage they may use strategies such as talking themselves through problems or counting by using their fingers as aids. Finally such aids are internalized, and except in cases of great difficulty problem solving thought uses internal dialogue, while language can be used to reflect on and develop thought rather than as a prop to support problem solving. Language also changes immediate perception and action, which become more and more integrated into a cognitive system that is to a large extent represented through language and expressed in language.

There is still, incidentally, considerable controversy about the developmental relationship of cognition and language (Goodluck, 1991). A full discussion of this (or of language development itself) is beyond the scope of this chapter. However, cognition might play a role in the development of language. It has been argued that cognition is necessary for language, and therefore that children cannot use a linguistic form until they understand the cognitive point that it relates to; but there are quite frequent instances, both in normal development and in certain pathological conditions, of correct syntax or vocabulary use coupled with failure on tests of the concept involved (Cramer, 1991), and of bilingual children expressing a concept correctly in one language but not in the other (Slobin, 1985).

It has alternatively been argued that language is "modularized", that an innate Language Acquisition Device programs language development, and cognitive development is of only marginal importance (Chomsky, 1968; Fodor, 1983; Karmiloff-Smith, 1991). Researchers agree that there is genetic programming underlying some aspects of language development, for example in infants' early phonetic discrimination and also, perhaps, in children's syntactic and semantic development (Cromer, 1991; Gleitman & Wanner, 1982; Pinker, 1984); but Chomsky's argument rests on an underestimation of the variation in human language behaviour. Since the 1980s studies have emphasized the role of social interaction in language development, particularly the facilitating effects of the use of child-contingent language by adults talking with children (Dickinson & McCabe, 1991; Heath, 1983; Meadows, 1986; Okagaki & Sternberg, 1991; Wells, 1985).

This "fit" between adult and child language closely resembles Vygotskian scaffolding; it is worth noting, very briefly, that the differences of emphasis between a neo-Vygotskian approach, emphasizing how embedded cognitive functioning is in social experience, on the one hand, and the asocial information-processing approach and the individualism of Piaget's work on the other, parallel these differences of emphasis in work on language development. Both cognition and language include behaviour that is clearly influenced by social interaction (for example the skills of literacy) and other skills that are less socialized (for example memory). These areas are discussed below.

Vygotsky's emphasis on social interaction implies that more complex cognitive functioning may be possible in a dialogue between cooperating individuals than is possible for those individuals alone, thus that the level of an individual's functioning may depend on the social support currently available for cognition, and, very importantly, that instruction may be a facilitator of cognitive development rather than the irrelevance or the distortion that the Piagetian model suggests (Hinde et al., 1985; Meadows, 1993).

THEORIES AND ISSUES IN THE DEVELOPMENT OF COGNITIVE SKILLS

How do the three theoretical approaches described above appear in the light of data on children's cognitive behaviour at different points in development? They are not mutually exclusive; indeed there are some very interesting models of cognitive development that combine approaches, notably the work of Karmiloff-Smith (1986, 1991). I have already argued that each has strengths and weaknesses, and that different areas of "cognition" seem to bear different emphases. I shall now describe two major and contrasting areas of cognition, first memory, which is essential for all learning, is largely untaught and could be considered to be basically a biologically programmed capacity with a long evolutionary history and subject to only minor cultural modifications, and second, literacy, which although it comes to pervade much of the cognition of the literate and uses biologically based capacities, is clearly a major focus of educational effort and acculturation, and has not existed long or widely enough to be subject to much evolutionary selection. The skills of memory are more "natural", while those of literacy are a matter of "nurture"; comparing the two will illuminate the debate on the universality and generality of cognitive development and on what its causes are.

Memory development

The information-processing approach, which has dominated the study of memory, suggests four main candidates for the locus of development: the size of the memory, basic memory processes, strategies for remembering, and metamemory. It remains possible that the size of the memory stores increases as children grow older, though it has been impossible so far to separate change in capacity (argued for by the Piagetian information-processors Pascual-Leone and Case) from change in how much can be squeezed into an unchanging capacity as memory processes become quicker, more effective, and more automatic (Meadows, 1993). Certainly the amount of information known and rememberable increases enormously with development; certainly, too, neurons in the brain can form new interconnections throughout life, so that connectionist pathways continue to develop.

It appears that quite young infants are capable of feats of memory which suggest that basic processes are operating from the earliest months of life: they can habituate, recognize faces and voices, learn the contingencies between their own movements and those of a mobile, and so forth (Butterworth, 1993). Many memories persist for long periods of time in early childhood, though they may become less accessible as older children reinterpret and reorganize their knowledge. Changes in the knowledge base may occasionally lead to an improvement in memory, through a new understanding of what was known earlier (Piaget, 1983).

There certainly are changes in the use of memory strategies, with a major increase in the frequency and the efficiency of their use over the school years. Young children may remember things well, but they rarely use overt memory strategies (except in well-understood games such as hide-and-seek); deliberate memorization emerges in the early school years. What happens fits a Vygotskian pattern as culturally given strategies become superimposed on biologically programmed ones, with a resultant transformation in performance. Training in the laboratory, which highlights the better remembering that rehearsal, categorization, elaboration, or other memory strategies can bring about, may induce a persistent use of memory strategies; analogous experiences may occur during everyday domestic routines such as shopping, or in the early years of schooling. Finally there is improvement in metamemory, as children become more able to identify with certainty what they do and do not know, what their cognitive strengths and weaknesses are, what improves and what impedes their remembering, and how their current study is progressing at each moment. Here Vygotskian internalization, Piagetian reflection, and information-processing executive strategies would seem to be overlapping descriptions and explanations of the child's behaviour.

Becoming literate

Becoming literate is a central part of cognitive development for several reasons: literacy involves many linguistic, perceptual, attentional, memory, and cognitive skills; its development illustrates the variety of developmental processes; achieving an adequate degree of literacy is one of the prime aims of many educational systems; and literacy itself may determine what cognitive skills can be used even on tasks that do not directly involve being literate. A further reason why it is of particular interest is that a combination of careful experimental work and large sample assessment in schoolchildren has led us to a much more accurate understanding of what children do when they read and write, and hence to more understanding of how they may be taught (Goswami & Bryant, 1990; Meadows, 1993).

Children beginning to learn to read have behind them years of experience of spoken language, of visual and auditory discrimination, of remembering pieces of information until they build up into a meaningful whole, of obtaining information from a range of sources. Their task is now to apply these linguistic and cognitive skills to written text. Children who lack any of these skills to a significant degree have more difficulty in becoming literate than those who are more skilled. Expert readers do most of their reading by a combination of recognizing overlearned familiar words and the expectations as to probable content that their knowledge of the current topic and of text in general affords them (Ellis & Young, 1988). Beginning readers similarly learn to recognize familiar words and to guess from the context of topic and pictures. These strategies are not much use with unrecognizable words; but if these words are in the child's spoken vocabulary (and for a young child the spoken vocabulary will be considerably larger than the sight vocabulary) they will be identifiable if the child has a strategy that gives a sounded-out version of the written word.

It is at this point of linking written word with sound that many children have problems. The ability to discriminate between different speech sounds, in particular, has been shown to be a crucial component of progress in reading beyond the earliest stage when words are recognized as familiar patterns (Goswami & Bryant, 1990); children who cannot work out how an unrecognized written word would sound have only a very restricted access to its meaning (by guessing, which may be unreliable, or by asking a more expert reader, which may not be allowed) and are likely to make poor progress in learning to read. This lack of progress may in turn lead to such undesirable consequences as reading less, rarely using reading for either amusement or information, public and humiliating failure in school, falling behind in other areas of the curriculum where reading is necessary, loss of self-confidence and motivation to learn, and so forth. There are many useful strategies for reading, but the strategy of linking of seen and sounded words is a particularly important one between the earliest reading of a few familiar words and the expert stage when most words are familiar: at that stage it reduces memory load and eases recognition.

DOMAINS OF COGNITIVE DEVELOPMENT

The theoretical approaches of Piaget and information-processing researchers assumed that thinking and its development are essentially the same across all areas. Vygotsky, too, discussed very general forms of cognitive development, though his greater stress on acculturation admitted the possibility of much more variation in cognition. Later, there has been more research that looked at the different structures of understanding that build up in different "domains" of knowledge, and it has been claimed that cognition is to some extent "modularized", that is, that conceptual understanding of one domain may be quite different in its form, its origins, and its development from understanding of another domain. This focus admits that there may indeed be general abstract high-level cognitive processes (such as assimilation or internalization or categorization), which the domain-general approaches asserted were important, but that there are many examples of very localized cognitive expertise, where a high degree of skill is tied to particular content. Studies such as that of Chi (1978) on the memory of chess players and of Ceci (1990) on race-course handicappers illustrate this.

"Domain" refers to localized areas of cognition where processes and concepts form a fairly coherent whole, less closely related to other domains. There are some suggestions of innate or genetically programmed modules, which operate with minimal environmental support, for example a specialized faculty for language and language acquisition (Anderson, 1992; Chomsky, 1968; Fodor, 1983); others are areas of acquired expertise, such as the ability to write computer programs, which is the result of prolonged and intensive experience. Other sorts of domains that have been a focus of attention are the "naive" or "common sense" theories that divide our rich day-to-day experience into organized systems of knowledge, linking together particular sorts of event or concept as parts of the same domain. There seems to be, for example, a basic ontological distinction between people, other living things, and inanimate objects in most people's everyday understanding.

It seems that infants and children very rapidly develop basic understandings of the world which observe these ontological distinctions and which develop with time into the sorts of "folk" theories of psychology, biology and physics that adults use (Carey, 1991; Gelman, 1991; Perner, 1991). Research on the child's "theory of mind" suggests that by the age of 3 to 4 years they understand that people (but not inanimate objects) have desires and beliefs, and that the latter can be objectively false; these understandings arise from the social interactions of infancy, perhaps from a biologically programmed module (Anderson, 1992), but amount by the fourth year to a complex model of other people's mental lives. Similarly, notions of what objects are like in physical terms and of physical causality begin in infancy and develop in a coherent, if technically inadequate, theory of causation; and biology becomes increasingly clearly differentiated from both psychology and physics as ideas about growth, inheritance, and what it is to be alive become more and more refined.

The child's understanding of all these domains has early roots, followed by a long development, and is not necessarily correct, not even as correct as that of adults; the argument of theorists studying these sorts of domains is that theories that have a fair degree of internal coherence guide the classification of experience and the development of knowledge. The child has a notion of causality, for example, which can underpin performance on analogical reasoning tasks (Goswami & Brown, 1990) that are much more difficult if the basis for the analogy is non-causal, such as a semantic opposition. Children's basic understandings will allow them to give answers that are correct in principle even when their ignorance means that they are wrong about detail, as in their early appeal to a story character's beliefs as a reason for their actions, even when the only details they can give about the beliefs are vague or incorrect. Much work in this field is demonstrating earlier competence than the traditional approaches which deliberately used more abstract, formal content.

SOURCES OF INDIVIDUAL DIFFERENCES IN COGNITIVE DEVELOPMENT

All the work discussed so far looks for a single general path of cognitive development, attending only to differences that are age-related. It is perhaps assumed that a "normal" pattern of development has to be discovered before any exceptions to it can usefully be studied; or even that exceptions are non-existent or pathological, as in some Piagetian and information-processing work. If the possibility that cognition is domain-specific and culturally constituted is taken seriously, and it has to be if such cognitive tools as reading are to be studied, then there is far more obvious variation between individuals in cognitive development, and a consequent need to chart the causes of this variation. Elucidating the causes of individual differences will, I would argue, clarify the causes of "normal" development.

One possibility as a source of individual differences is that they are genetic, that is, that an innate variation in the individual's genetic programming leads, not necessarily directly or independently of other influences, to a particular form of cognitive development, just as genetic programming leads to differences in eye colour or number of toes. It is clear that certain major genetic anomalies cause abnormalities of brain development or functioning which lead to abnormal cognitive development; Down's Syndrome and Turner's Syndrome are examples where an abnormal amount of genetic material leads to the development of a child who has a number of physical and cognitive abnormalities. If a markedly wrong gene "messes up" (Scarr & Carter-Saltzman, 1982) the program for cognitive development, then it could be that smaller variations also have genetic roots, that subtler genetic peculiarities lead to subtler cognitive differences.

Exactly this argument appears in the study of "intelligence" (Anderson, 1992; Eysenck, 1982; Meadows, 1993); for example it is suggested that some brains are innately "faster" or "more efficient" in their basic processing because of their owners' comparatively favourable genes, and that therefore those individuals may think and learn better than individuals with "slower" brain speeds. Undoubtedly cognition depends on brain functioning, and this is to a considerable extent the result of a genetic program of development; but neuroscience is demonstrating that brain functioning, structure, and biochemistry are also the result of experience and learning continuing over the years of childhood and beyond (Greenough & Black, 1992; Meadows, 1993), and it may be more fruitful to look at differences in *experience* when searching for sources of individual differences in cognitive development.

To do this requires a much better conceptualization of what is relevant "experience" than any current theoretical perspective affords. The relevant experiences will be both physical and social. Several aspects of the physical environment are suspected of being damaging to cognitive development (Meadows, 1993), including various sorts of pollution and dietary deficiencies. The causal sequences are not yet perfectly clear, but nervous system damage and impairment of attention and motivation may be involved. Severe prenatal malnutrition, for example, may reduce the number of brain cells that develop, and this reduction may be handicapping in later cognitive development, though the evidence is not entirely clear; severe malnutrition in childhood certainly has adverse effects on health and energy which impede involvement in the exploration and education that normally lead to good cognitive development.

The brain is affected by environmental factors throughout life, as brain development continues throughout childhood, and new neural connections can be formed and lost throughout life. During the early years, there are periods of rapid proliferation of nerve cell connections followed by the selective dying-off of connections that have served no useful purpose; later development is a matter of the rearrangement of connections as new links supersede old ones, rather than of enormous increases in connectivity. Current work in developmental neuropsychology is transforming our understanding of the links between brain development and cognitive development in both normal and abnormal development, and a complex and exciting picture is emerging (for an introduction, see Meadows, 1993).

Studies of the effects of the social environment on cognitive development are not likely to provide a simpler set of influences than studies of the physical environment, and are complicated by the lack of an adequate grasp of how the social environment should be described and assessed (Meadows, 1993). Variables such as social class are associated with differences in cognitive development as assessed by school achievement, but do not indicate at all clearly what causes the association. The best candidate for social experience affecting cognitive development that a theory offers is Vygotsky's idea of "scaffolding" (Meadows, 1993; Tharp & Gallimore, 1988; Wood, 1988).

There have been several demonstrations that teaching problem solving in a Vygotskian manner facilitates children's performance on that problem and, perhaps, their ability to transfer what they have learned to another problem (Tharp & Gallimore, 1988; Wertsch, McNamee, McLane, & Budwid, 1980; Wood, 1988). Language development is similarly facilitated by Vygotskian child-contingent language (Wells, 1987). There is some evidence that parenting that is notably lacking in scaffolding and child-contingent discussion is associated with later difficulties in concentration and the development and elaboration of activities (Meadows, 1993). However, we know very little about how common scaffolding is in adults' dealings with children; whether more is better, or whether there is an "enough is as good as a feast" effect; whether the cultural differences that appear in language development apply also in cognition; whether there are alternative ways of getting the same good result (and it does seem clear that some cultures do not engage in what is recognized as scaffolding in Anglo-American settings); and whether there are stable differences between individuals in how much scaffolding they need for optimum development. Further, we do not know how scaffolding affects the child; it may provide models of cognitive skills, or of self-scaffolding, or encouragement, or lower failure rates, or a transformation of failure into a good opportunity to learn, or all of these: in other words, there may be a multitude of cognitive or motivational effects. One interesting prediction from the Vygotskian model is that the recipients of successful scaffolding not only may learn the tasks in question but also may learn to scaffold themselves through new learning, perhaps turning, effectively, into Piagetian learners. Further research is necessary to sort out these issues. So is further development of theory, beyond the assumption that cognition can be studied as independent of affect, motivation, and the social world.

FURTHER READING

Goodluck, H. (1991). *Language acquisition*. Oxford: Basil Blackwell.
Meadows, S. (1993). *The child as thinker: The acquisition and development of cognitive skills in childhood*. London: Routledge.

REFERENCES

Anderson, M. (1992). *Intelligence and cognitive development*. Oxford: Basil Blackwell.

Azmitia, M., & Perlmutter, M. (1989). Social influences on young children's cognition: State of the art and future directions. In H. W. Reese (Ed.) *Advances in child development and behavior* (vol. 22, pp. 90–145). New York: Wiley.

Beilin, H. (1992). Piaget's enduring contribution to developmental psychology. *Developmental Psychology, 28,* 191–204.

Bronfenbrenner, U. (1979). *The ecology of human development*. Cambridge, MA: Harvard University Press.

Bryant, P. (1985). Parents, children and cognitive development. In R. Hinde, A.-N. Perret-Clermont, & J. Stevenson-Hinde (Eds) *Social relationships and cognitive development* (pp. 239–251). Cambridge: Cambridge University Press.

Butterworth, G. (1994). *Infancy*. In A. M. Colman (Ed.) *Companion encyclopedia of psychology* (pp. 683–698). London: Routledge.

Carey, S. (1991). Knowledge acquisition: Enrichment or conceptual change. In S. Carey & R. Gelman (Eds) *The epigenesis of mind* (pp. 257–291). Hove: Lawrence Erlbaum.

Case, R. (1985). *Intellectual development: Birth to adulthood*. New York: Academic Press.

Ceci, S. (1990). *On intelligence... more or less: A bio-ecological theory of intellectual development*. New York: Prentice-Hall.

Chi, M. (1978). Knowledge structures and memory development. In R. S. Siegler (Ed.) *Children's thinking: What develops?* (pp. 73–96). Hillsdale, NJ: Lawrence Erlbaum.

Chi, M., & Ceci, S. (1987). Content knowledge: Its role, representation and restructuring in memory development. In H. W. Reese (Ed.) *Advances in child development and behaviour* (vol. 20, pp. 91–142). New York: Academic Press.

Chomsky, N. (1968). *Language and mind*. New York: Harcourt Brace Jovanovich.

Clark, A. (1989). *Microcognition: Philosophy, cognitive science and parallel distributed processing*. Cambridge, MA: Massachusetts Institute of Technology Press.

Cromer, R. (1991). *Language and thought in normal and handicapped children*. Oxford: Basil Blackwell.

Dickinson, D., & McCabe, A. (1991). The acquisition and development of language. In J. F. Kavanagh (Ed.) *The language continuum: From infancy to literacy* (pp. 1–40). Parkton, MD: York Press.

Donaldson, M. (1978). *Children's minds*. London: Fontana.

Ellis, A. W., & Young, A. W. (1988). *Human cognitive neuropsychology*. London: Lawrence Erlbaum.

Eysenck, H. (Ed.) (1982). *A model for intelligence*. Berlin: Springer.

Fodor, J. (1983). *The modularity of mind*. Cambridge, MA: Massachusetts Institute of Technology Press.

Gelman, R. (1991). Epigenetic foundations of knowledge structures: Initial and transcendent constructions. In S. Carey & R. Gelman (Eds) *The epigenesis of mind* (pp. 293–322). Hove: Lawrence Erlbaum.

Gleitman, L. R., & Wanner, E. (1982). Language acquisition: The state of the art. In E. Wanner & L. R. Gleitman (Eds) *Language acquisition: The state of the art* (pp. 3–50). Cambridge, MA: Harvard University Press.

Goodluck, H. (1991). *Language acquisition*. Oxford: Basil Blackwell.

Goswami, U., & Brown, A. L. (1990). Melting chocolate and melting snowmen: Analogical reasoning and causal relations. *Cognition, 35,* 69–96.

Goswami, U., & Bryant, P. (1990). *Phonological skills and learning to read.* Hove: Lawrence Erlbaum.

Greenough, W. T., & Black, J. E. (1992). Induction of brain structure by experience: Substrates for cognitive development. In M. Gunnar & C. A. Nelson (Eds) *Developmental behavioral neuroscience. Minnesota symposium on child development, 24,* 155–200.

Harris, P. (1983). Infant cognition. In M. M. Haith & J. J. Campos (Eds) *Handbook of child psychology* (vol. 2, pp. 689–782). New York: Wiley.

Heath, S. B. (1983). *Ways with words.* Cambridge: Cambridge University Press.

Hinde, R., Perret-Clermont, A.-N., & Stevenson-Hinde, J. (Eds) (1985). *Social relationships and cognitive development.* Oxford: Oxford University Press.

Kail, R. (1991). Developmental change in speed of processing during childhood and adolescence. *Psychological Bulletin, 109,* 490–501.

Karmiloff-Smith, A. (1986). From meta-processes to conscious access: Evidence from children's metalinguistics and repair data. *Cognition, 23,* 95–147.

Karmiloff-Smith, A. (1991). Beyond modularity: Innate constraints and developmental change. In S. Carey & R. Gelman (Eds) *The epigenesis of mind* (pp. 171–197). Hillsdale, NJ: Lawrence Erlbaum.

Keil, F. (1989). *Concepts, kinds and cognitive development.* Boston, MA: Massachusetts Institute of Technology Press.

Kozulin, A. (1990). *Vygotsky's psychology.* Brighton: Harvester.

Light, P. (1986). Context, conservation and conversation. In M. Richards & P. Light (Eds) *Children of social worlds* (pp. 170–190). Cambridge: Polity.

McClelland, J. L., Rumelhart, D. E., & the PDP Research Group (1986). *Parallel distributed processing: Explorations in the micro-structure of cognition, vol. 2. Psychological and biological models.* Cambridge, MA: Massachusetts Institute of Technology Press.

McShane, J. (1991). *Cognitive development: An information-processing approach.* Oxford: Basil Blackwell.

Meadows, S. (1986). *Understanding child development.* London: Hutchinson.

Meadows, S. (1993). *The child as thinker: The acquisition and development of cognition in childhood.* London: Routledge.

Okagaki, L., & Sternberg, R. J. (Eds) (1991). *Directors of development: Influences on the development of children's thinking.* Hillsdale, NJ: Lawrence Erlbaum.

Perner, J. (1991). *Understanding the representational mind.* Cambridge, MA: Massachusetts Institute of Technology Press.

Piaget, J. (1983). Piaget's theory. In P. H. Mussen (Ed.) *Handbook of child psychology* (vol. 3, pp. 103–128). New York: Wiley.

Pinker, S. (1984). *Language learnability and language development.* Cambridge, MA: Harvard University Press.

Scarr, S., & Carter-Saltzman, L. (1982). Genetics and intelligence. In R. Sternberg (Ed.) *Handbook of human intelligence* (pp. 792–896). Cambridge, MA: Cambridge University Press.

Siegel, M. (1991). *Knowing children: Experiments in conversation and cognition.* Hove: Lawrence Erlbaum.

Siegler, R. (1983). Information-processing approaches to development. In W. Kessen (Ed.) *Handbook of child psychology* (vol. 1, pp. 129–212). New York: Wiley.

Siegler, R. (1986). *Children's thinking.* Englewood Cliffs, NJ: Prentice-Hall.

Slobin, D. I. (Ed.) (1985). *The cross linguistic study of language acquisition.* Hillsdale, NJ: Lawrence Erlbaum.

Smedslund, J. (1980). Analyzing the primary code: From empiricism to apriorism. In D. R. Olson (Ed.) *The social foundations of language and thought* (pp. 47–73). New York: Norton.

Sternberg, R. J. (Ed.) (1984). *Mechanisms of cognitive development*. New York: Freeman.

Tharp, R., & Gallimore, R. (1988). *Rousing minds to life: Teaching, learning and schooling in social context*. Cambridge: Cambridge University Press.

Vygotsky, L. S. (1978). *Mind in society: The development of higher psychological processes*. Cambridge, MA: Harvard University Press.

Vygotsky, L. S. (1986). *Thought and language*. Cambridge, MA: Harvard University Press.

Wells, G. (1987). *The meaning makers*. Sevenoaks: Hodder & Stoughton.

Wertsch, J. V., McNamee, G. D., McLane, J. B. & Budwid, N. A. (1980). The adult–child dyad as a problem-solving system. *Child Development*, *51*, 1215–1221.

Wood, D. J. (1988). *How children think and learn*. Oxford: Basil Blackwell.

3

SOCIAL DEVELOPMENT

Peter K. Smith
University of Sheffield, England

During the years of infancy, social development takes place primarily with parents and adult caregivers. From birth and soon afterwards, babies possess reflexive abilities and learning capacities that assist the development of social interchanges with adults. They preferentially focus on the kinds of visual and auditory stimuli that adults typically provide when talking, and when putting their face close to an infant. Also, they enjoy the kinds of contingent responsiveness that are generally obtained from adults, for example, vocalizing when they coo or babble, cuddling them when they cry.

Some psychologists, such as Trevarthen (1977), strongly emphasize the early abilities of rhythm and intersubjectivity that the infant brings to these social interchanges. Others, such as Kaye (1984), rather emphasize the limited abilities of the infant in the first year of life, and the role of the adult caregiver in "scaffolding" the interactions by providing the right response to

34

whatever the infant does, and timing responses appropriately to mesh in with the infant's timing. Certainly, the infant will be learning a great deal over the first 12 to 18 months, through observation and imitation.

Infants will also be learning to discriminate between different adults and caregivers, and typically are becoming attached to a small number of these towards the end of the first year. Despite evidence for some discrimination much earlier, the obvious signs of preferring a familiar caregiver to a stranger, and being reassured by the former but not by the latter, usually appear from 7 months on. This process of attachment has been described in detail by Bowlby (1969); he argues that the attachment system functions to provide a secure base for the infant to explore the physical and social environment. If alarmed or stressed, the infant will return to seek the proximity and reassurance of the attachment figure.

Some attachment theorists, such as Ainsworth, Blehar, Waters, and Wall (1978), and Main (1991), distinguish between secure and insecure attachment. A securely attached infant, when distressed, is reassured by the attachment figure. An insecurely attached infant, when distressed, will show some ambivalence to, or avoidance of, the attachment figure, or may show a dis-organized response. These patterns of attachment (which measure a relation-ship between an infant and a particular caregiver) are measured by a procedure called the "strange situation", which re-enacts in miniature a situ-ation involving an infant being mildly stressed by being left with a stranger, and assessing response to the caregiver on her or his return (Ainsworth et al., 1978). This procedure is applicable to infants aged 1 to 3 years. Beyond that age, attachment theorists prefer to talk about "internal working models" of relationships, which can be assessed by different means in middle childhood, and through to adulthood (Main, 1991).

Despite an earlier misplaced emphasis by Bowlby (1953) on the unique importance of mothers as attachment figures, it is now generally accepted that attachment figures can include fathers, grandparents, older siblings, and familiar non-family adults such as nannies or childminders; and that a child can be attached to several such persons. This recognition has to some extent defused the long-running controversy about whether infants can be left in non-family day-care situations without any adverse effects. It is generally felt that there are no necessary adverse effects consequent upon high-quality day-care (Clarke-Stewart, 1989), though some uncertainty still remains about the effects of intensive, early day-care on the quality of mother–infant attachment (Belsky, 1988).

EARLY PEER RELATIONSHIPS

By the age of 2 years, peers – other children of about the same age – become increasing sources of interest. In fact, peers seem to be especially interesting to children even in the second year of life. In one study of 12–18-month-old infants, two mother–infant pairs who had not previously met shared a play-room together. The infants touched their mothers a lot (remaining in prox-imity to them, as we would expect from attachment theory), but *looked* most at the peer, who clearly interested them (Lewis, Young, Brooks, & Michalson, 1975).

The interactions between under-2s often consist of just looking at another child and perhaps smiling, or showing a toy, or making a noise. In toddler groups an infant might make such overtures to another child once every minute or so, and any interactions are brief (Mueller & Brenner, 1977). This rather low level of peer interaction is probably because infants have not yet learned the skills of social interaction. Whereas adults can "scaffold" social interactions with infants, it takes young children some 2 or 3 years to become really competent at interacting socially with age-mates, knowing what are appropriate behaviours in certain situations, what behaviour to expect back, and waiting to take one's turn. There is some evidence that early peer experi-ence (e.g., in toddler groups or day nurseries) can help this along. Some studies suggest that infants who are "securely attached" to their mothers are more confident and better able to explore both objects and peers, and to make new social relationships over the next few years (Bretherton & Waters, 1985; Turner, 1991).

SIBLINGS

The majority of us have siblings – brothers or sisters. Usually, siblings differ in age by only a few years. Although not exactly peers, they are generally close enough in age, and similar enough in interests and developmental stages, to be important social partners for each other in the family. Older siblings can show great tolerance for younger ones, and can act as important models for more competent behaviour. They can also show hostility and ambivalence; this has been observed in many different societies (Eibl-Eibesfeldt, 1989).

Dunn and Kendrick (1982) made observations in the homes of 40 firstborn children living with both parents in or near Cambridge, England. At first visit, a new sibling was due in a month or so, and the first child was usually nearing his or her second birthday. After the birth of the sibling they made further visits, when the second child was about 1 month old, and again at 8 months and at 14 months.

They found that many firstborns showed some signs of jealousy when the new sibling arrived. Although they had previously been the centre of atten-tion from mother, father, or grandparents, the new brother or sister now got the most attention. Much of the jealousy and ambivalence of the firstborn was directed towards parents. Not many firstborns showed much overt hostility to the infant, but some showed ambivalence or hostility, as the fol-lowing extract of conversation shows:

Child: Baby, baby (caressing her). Monster. Monster.
Mother: She's not a monster.
Child: Monster.

However, the great majority of the firstborns showed much interest and affection towards their new siblings seeking to please them, or being concerned if they cried. Overall, Dunn and Kendrick (1982) felt that the sibling relationship was one in which considerable emotions may be aroused – both of love and of envy.

This close and emotionally powerful relationship may also be an optimal situation in which to learn how to understand others. Siblings seem to be learning how to frustrate, tease, placate, comfort, or get their own way with their brother or sister. Dunn and Kendrick (1982) relate one incident in which 14-month-old Callum repeatedly reaches for and manipulates some magnetic letters which his 3-year-old sister Laura is playing with on a tray. Laura repeatedly says "no" gently. Callum continues trying to reach the letters. Finally, Laura picks up the tray with the letters and takes it to a high table that Callum cannot reach. Callum is furious and starts to cry. He turns and goes straight to the sofa where Laura's comfort objects, a rag doll and a pacifier, are lying. He takes the doll and holds it tight, looking at Laura. Laura now gets very upset, starts crying, and runs to take the doll.

Callum seems to have calculated how to annoy Laura so as to get his own back on her. These are interesting observations to compare with ideas about children's "theory of mind", as well as the critique of Piaget's ideas about egocentrism. But it is also worth bearing in mind that children can learn these social-cognitive skills with adults and peers, as well as with siblings. Research on only children appears to suggest that they do well on achievement and intelligence scores, and show no deficits in sociability or adjustment (Falbo & Polit, 1986).

THE SCHOOL YEARS

By 2 or 3 years of age a child is usually thought to be ready for nursery school. The period from 2 to 4 years does see a great increase in the skills children have with peers. Sociodramatic play (pretend role-play with others) and rough-and-tumble play (friendly play-fighting with a partner) become frequent in this age range. The child is also beginning to develop concrete operational thought and to be able to take the perspective of others in simple ways.

The increase in social behaviour in pre-school children was first documented by Parten (1932). She observed 2–4 year olds and described how they might be "unoccupied", an "onlooker" on others' activities, or, if engaged in an activity, they could be "solitary", in "parallel" activity with others, or in "associative" or "cooperative" activity with others. Parallel activity is when children play near each other with the same materials, but do not interact much – playing independently at the same sandpit for example. Associative activity is when children interact together at an activity, doing similar things, perhaps each adding building blocks to the same tower. Cooperative activity is when children interact together in complementary ways; for example, one child gets blocks out of a box and hands them to another child, who builds the tower. Parten found that the first four categories declined with age, whereas associative and cooperative activity, the only ones involving much interaction with peers, increased with age.

Most group activity involves just two or three children playing together, though the size of groups tends to increase in older pre-schoolers and in the early school years. A study of more than 400 Israeli children in outdoor free play found that group activity predominated, while parallel activity became very infrequent; the number of groups comprised of more than five children increased from 12 to 16 per cent between 5 and 6 years of age (Hertz-Lazarowitz, Feitelson, Zahavi, & Hartup, 1981). The size of children's groups continues to increase through the middle school years (about 9–12 years old), especially in boys, as team games such as football become more popular. The nature of children's groups changes again as adolescence is reached, when large same-sex cliques or gangs become common in early adolescence, changing as heterosexual relationships become more important in later adolescence.

CONCEPTIONS OF FRIENDSHIP

Usually we take friendship to mean some close association between two particular people, as indicated by their association together or their psychological attachment and trust. It is quite possible to interact a lot with others generally but not have any close friends.

How do children themselves conceive of friendship? Bigelow and La Gaipa (1980) asked Scottish and Canadian children, aged 6 to 14 years, to write an essay about their expectations of best friends. Based on a content analysis, Bigelow and La Gaipa suggested a three-stage model for friendship expectations. A "reward-cost" stage, based on common activities, living nearby, having similar expectations, was common up to 8 years. From 9 to 10 years, a "normative" stage emphasized shared values, rules, and sanctions. At 11–12 years, an "empathic" stage showed a more mature conception of friendship based on understanding, and self-disclosure, as well as shared interests. These and other studies suggest a shift towards more psychologically complex and mutually reciprocal ideas of friendship during the middle school years, with intimacy and commitment becoming especially important later in adolescence.

THE MEASUREMENT OF FRIENDSHIP: SOCIOMETRY

It is possible to build up a picture of the social structure in a group of children using a technique called sociometry. This can be done by observation. Clark, Wyon, and Richards (1969) observed nursery school children to record who was playing with whom, at intervals over a five-week period. They constructed *sociograms* (an example is shown in Figure l). Each symbol represents a child; the thickness of lines joining two children represents the percentage of observations on which they were seen playing together. The concentric circles show the number of play partners a child has: if many, that child's symbol is towards the middle, if none, at the periphery. In this class there is one very popular girl who links two large subgroups; one boy and one girl have no clear partners.

Observation shows who associates with whom, but this may not be quite the same as friendship. An alternative is to ask each child "Who are your best friends?" The nomination data can also be plotted on a sociogram. If John chooses Richard as a best friend, but Richard does not choose John, this can

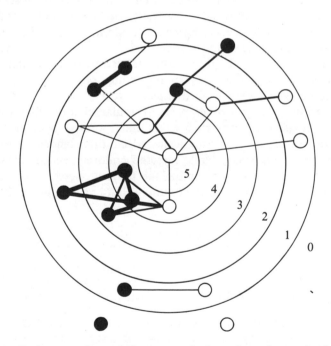

Figure 1 Sociogram of association networks in a class of pre-school children
Source: Adapted from Clark, Wyon, and Richards, 1969
Note: White circles represent girls, black circles represent boys

be indicated by an arrow from John to Richard; if the choice is reciprocated, the arrow would point both ways on the sociogram.

A common nomination method is to ask each child to name their three best friends. Some investigators have also asked children to say whom they do not like. There may be ethical objections to this (for example, such questions actually might bring about increased negative behaviour to unliked peers) but so far ill effects have not been found (Hayvren & Hymel, 1984). Researchers who have obtained both positive and negative nominations have not constructed sociograms (which would then look very complicated), but have instead categorized children as "popular", "controversial", "rejected", "neglected", or "average", according to whether they are high or low on positive and on negative nominations (see Table 1).

Coie and Dodge (1983) looked at the stability of these sociometric status categories between 8 and 11 years. They found that stability was highest for "rejected" children; 30 per cent of those rejected at 8 years were still rejected four years later, and another 30 per cent were "neglected". By contrast, those merely "neglected" at the start of the study tended to become "average".

Rejected children do seem to differ in their behaviour from most other children, in what seem to be maladaptive ways. Ladd (1983) observed 8 and 9 year olds in playground breaks. Rejected children, compared to average or popular children, spent less time in cooperative play and social conversation, and more time arguing and fighting, they tended to play in smaller groups, and with younger or with less popular companions. Dodge, Schlundt, Shocken, & Delugach (1983) looked at how 5 year olds attempted to get into ongoing play between two other peers. Popular children first waited and watched, then gradually got themselves incorporated by making group-oriented statements; by contrast, neglected children tended to stay at the waiting and watching stage, while rejected children tended to escalate to disruptive actions such as interrupting the play.

Children who are rejected in the middle school years (ages 9–12) may be

Table 1 Five types of sociometric status

POPULAR High on "liked most" Low on "liked least"	CONTROVERSIAL High on "liked most" High on "liked least"
AVERAGE	
NEGLECTED Low on "liked most" Low on "liked least"	REJECTED Low on "liked most" High on "liked least"

more in need of help even than those who simply keep a low profile and are ignored or neglected. The findings above suggest that rejected children are lacking in some social skills. This is a widely held view, and has been developed by Dodge, Pettit, McClaskey, & Brown (1986). They suggest that the social skills of peer interaction can be envisaged as an exchange model (see Figure 2). Suppose child A is interacting with child B. According to this model she has to (1) encode the incoming information – perceive what child B is doing, (2) interpret this information, (3) search for appropriate responses, (4) evaluate these responses and select the best, and (5) enact that response. Child B will be engaged in a similar process with respect to child A.

This model may be helpful in making the term "social skills" more explicit. If a child has a social skills deficit, where is this located? Does an over-aggressive child misinterpret others' behaviour (stage 2), or just too readily select aggressive responses (stage 4), for example?

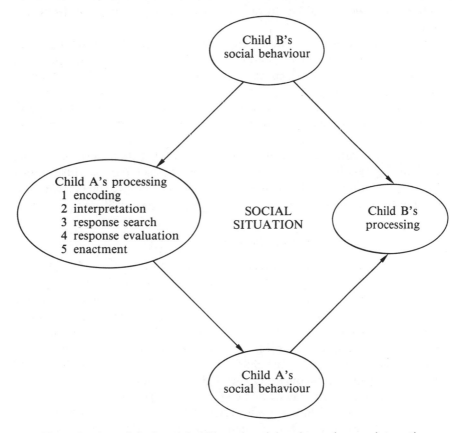

Figure 2 A model of social skills and social exchange in peer interaction
Source: Adapted from Dodge, Pettit, McClaskey, and Brown, 1986

However, not all behaviour labelled as maladjusted may be due to *lack* of social skills. Some aggressive children may be quite skilled at manipulating others. And some rejected children may be simply reacting to exclusion by the popular cliques and would not necessarily be rejected or lacking in social skills in other situations outside the classroom.

THE IMPORTANCE OF FRIENDSHIP

It seems likely that having friends is important for a child's development, but it is difficult to prove this. Parker and Asher (1987) reviewed many relevant studies, most carried out in the USA. They looked at three measures of peer relationships: peer acceptance/rejection (number and quality of friendships); aggressiveness to peers; and shyness or withdrawal from peers. They examined the relationship of these to three main kinds of later outcome: dropping out of school early; being involved in juvenile and adult crime; and adult psychopathology (mental health ratings, or needing psychiatric help of any kind).

They found a consistent link between low peer acceptance (or high peer rejection) and dropping out of school, and a suggestive link with juvenile/adult crime. There was also a consistent link between aggressiveness at school and juvenile/adult crime, with a suggestive link with dropping out of school. The data on effects of shyness/withdrawal, and on predictors of adult psychopathology, were less consistent, with any links or effects unproven at present.

Whatever the difficulties of proof, many psychologists believe that social skills training may be useful for those children who lack friends; this training is anyway usually directed to changing behaviours that are the correlates of peer rejection (such as high aggression, or high withdrawal).

SOCIAL SKILLS TRAINING

Attempts have been made by psychologists to help improve social skills in rejected or neglected children. Furman, Rahe, and Hartup (1979) observed 4 and 5 year olds who seldom played with other children. Some received special play sessions with a younger partner, to see if this might give them more confidence in social interaction. This did seem to help, more so than play sessions with a same-age peer or no intervention at all. Other researchers, working with middle-school-age children (about 9–12 years old), have used more direct means of encouraging social skills. A child might watch a film showing an initially withdrawn child engaged in a series of increasingly complex peer interactions. This has been shown to increase social interaction subsequently (O'Connor, 1972). Ogden and Asher (1977) used a more instructional approach, coaching 8- and 9-year-old children identified as socially isolated (neglected or rejected) on skills such as how to participate in groups, cooperate, and communicate with peers. They did this in special play sessions with the target child and one other peer. These children improved in sociometric status more than those who had special play sessions without the coaching.

FACTORS AFFECTING POPULARITY IN CHILDREN

Children differ in popularity and some less popular children may have less adequate social skills. But other factors are certainly at work. One such factor is physical attractiveness. Vaughn and Langlois (1983) obtained ratings of physical attractiveness for 59 pre-school children, and found a high correlation with sociometric preference. Other studies have found that ratings of physical attractiveness correlate with sociometric status.

Popularity may also be influenced by the composition of the peer group a child is in. Children tend to pick as friends peers similar to themselves. A child might tend to appear sociometrically neglected or rejected simply because he or she differs in social class, or ethnicity, from most others in the class.

AGGRESSION IN CHILDREN

It is not unusual for children to show aggression, and for young children this will often be shown in physical forms such us fighting, or in verbal taunts. Jersild and Markey (1935) observed conflicts in 54 children at three nursery schools, and described many kinds of conflict behaviour, such as taking or grabbing toys or objects held or used by another child and making unfavourable remarks about someone such as "You're no good at it" or "I don't like you". Some decline in conflicts occurred with age, and boys took part in more conflicts than girls. Nine months later, conflicts had become more verbal, but individual differences between children tended to be maintained. Cummings, Iannetti, and Zahn-Waxler (1989) similarly reported that aggressive boys tended to stay aggressive between 2 and 5 years of age, even though the overall level of physical aggression declined over this period.

Blurton Jones (1967) drew a clear distinction between physically aggressive behaviour, evidenced by beating or hitting at another with a frown or angry face, and rough-and-tumble play, where children chased and tackled each other, often smiling or laughing. These two kinds of behaviour can be confused because of their superficial similarity, but in fact most children are accomplished at telling them apart by at least 8 years of age (Costabile et al., 1991).

A number of researchers distinguish *verbal* and *non-verbal* aggression (based on the presence or absence of verbal threats or insults); *instrumental* and *hostile* aggression (based on whether the distress or harm is inferred to be the primary intent of the act); and *individual* and *group* aggression (depending on whether more than one child attacks another).

CAUSES OF HIGH AGGRESSION

A certain amount of aggressive and assertive behaviour is normal. However, some children show high levels of aggression, often of a hostile or harassing nature, which can be quite stable over time and for which some adult intervention seems justified. If not dealt with at the time, children who show persistent high aggressiveness through the school years are at increased risk for later delinquency, antisocial, and violent behaviour (Farrington, 1991).

There is considerable evidence that home circumstances can be important influences leading to aggressive and later antisocial behaviour. Patterson, DeBaryshe, and Ramsey (1989) suggest that certain key aspects of parenting are involved. Children who experience irritable and ineffective discipline at home, and poor parental monitoring of their activities, together with a lack of parental warmth, are particularly likely to become aggressive in peer groups and at school. Antisocial behaviour at school is likely to be linked to academic failure and peer rejection, they argue; and in adolescence, especially if parental monitoring is lax, these young people are likely to be involved in deviant and delinquent peer groups. Their hypothesis is shown in Figure 3.

This approach suggests that the social skills of *parenting* are very important in preventing antisocial behaviour; interventions can focus on helping parents improve their child-management skills, for example via manuals and videotaped materials.

Bullying in schools is one kind of persistent aggressive behaviour that can cause great distress to victims (Smith & Thompson, 1991). It can be carried out by one child, or a group, and is usually repeated against a particular victim. The victim usually cannot retaliate effectively. While some bullying

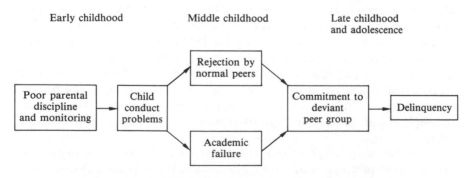

Figure 3 A developmental progression for antisocial behaviour
Source: Adapted from Patterson, DeBaryshe, and Ramsey, 1989

takes the form of hitting, pushing, taking money, it can also involve teasing, telling stories, and social exclusion. Research in western Europe suggests that bullying is quite pervasive in schools, probably to a greater extent than most teachers and parents realize, since many victims keep quiet about it. However, schools can take action to reduce the problem, by having definite "whole school" policies on the issue, improving playground supervision, raising awareness through curricular activities, and working intensively with individuals and small groups who are affected.

AGGRESSION, DOMINANCE, POPULARITY, AND LEADERSHIP

How does aggressive behaviour relate to popularity and leadership? One view is that aggressive children tend to be disliked and unpopular. Rejected children often show disruptive behaviour with peers, being disliked because of their unprovoked aggression. Some children, however, are quite aggressive but not clearly disliked. These are "controversial" children. Peers describe them as good leaders, but also as starting fights – a pattern of behaviour that appeals to some peers but not to others. Thus, some children may use aggressive behaviour in quite a socially skilled way, to acquire status in the peer group.

Sluckin (1981) made a detailed study of playground behaviour in an Oxford first school. He describes how a boy called Neill was known by his peers as the "boss" of the playground. Neill was seldom observed in actual fights (he was not physically strong), but he often tried to raise his prestige and manipulate social situations by verbal means. For example, in a race with Ginny, where they finished at the same time, Neill cried out "Yes, yes" (I'm the winner). Ginny called out "Draw", to which Neill replied "No, it wasn't, you're just trying to make trouble". Or, playing football, Neill said "I'm in goal, bagsee". Nick replied "No, I'm in goal". Neill retorted "No, John's in goal" and John went in the goal. Neill had kept the initiative, avoided a fight, but given the impression of being in charge (even though he did not get his own way entirely). Neill had a high-dominance status in the playground, and was clearly a leader of sorts, but was not especially popular. His leadership was often disruptive, since he always insisted on winning games.

Playground observations by Sluckin and others suggest that schoolchildren can rank others for dominance or fighting strength in a consistent way, and experiments confirm that this can be done reliably from about 4 or 5 years of age onwards (Sluckin & Smith, 1977). Winning fights is one criterion of dominance, but more generally it is taken as getting one's one way or influencing others. Thus, the concept is close to that of leadership.

In general, some children are popular, and often leaders, because they are socially skilled and assertive but not gratuitously aggressive. Another way of being a leader, or achieving high-dominance status, is to be a good fighter. This is a more controversial way, which may not bring true popularity with all one's peers. High aggression without the social skills to go with it, however, leads to unpopularity and rejection.

SEX DIFFERENCES AMONG CHILDREN

Up to 2 years there are not many consistent differences between girls and boys. The similarities certainly outweigh the dissimilarities; but girl infants may be more responsive to people, staying closer to adults, whereas boy infants may be more distressed by stressful situations that they cannot control. Girls also seem to talk earlier.

Observations of 2 year olds at home, and of 3 and 4 year olds in nursery classes, have found characteristic differences in choices of activity. Girls tend to prefer dolls, and dressing-up or domestic play; boys tend to prefer transportation toys, blocks, and activities involving gross motor activity such as throwing or kicking balls, or rough-and-tumbling. Many activities, however, do not show a sex preference at this age.

In nursery school children tend to select same-sex partners for play, and more so as they get older. By the time children are getting into team games from about 6 or 7 years onward, sex segregation in the playground is much greater. Girls prefer indoor, more sedentary activities, and often play in pairs; boys tend to prefer outdoor play and, later, team games. Girls tend to be more empathic, and remain more oriented towards adults (parents and teachers) longer into childhood; boys more frequently engage in both play-fighting and actual aggressive behaviour.

Lever (1978), in a study of 10–11-year-old children in American playgrounds, found that girls were more often in smaller groups of same-age pairs, while boys more often played in larger mixed-age groups. Girls put more emphasis on intimacy and exclusiveness in their friendships. Boys liked playing competitive team games that were more complex in their rules and role-structure, and that seemed to emphasize "political" skills of cooperation, competition,and leadership in their social relations.

STEREOTYPES OF SEX ROLES

Sex-role stereotypes are acquired early; these are beliefs about what is most appropriate for one sex, or the other. Kuhn, Nash, and Bruken (1978) showed pre-school children a female doll and a male doll, and asked which doll would do each of 72 activities, such as cooking, sewing, playing with trains, talking a lot, giving kisses, fighting, or climbing trees. Even $2\frac{1}{2}$ year olds had some knowledge of sex-role stereotypes (see Table 2). This sex-stereotyping increases with age and by the middle school years it is firmly established. In a study of 5- and 8-year-old children in England, Ireland, and the USA (Best et al, 1977), the majority of boys and girls agreed that females were soft-hearted whereas males were strong, aggressive, cruel, and coarse.

rd, children become able to think more flexibly about ethnic differences,
n terms of individuals rather than groups, so that their earlier prejudice
be modified.

hools have been a focus for work to reduce racial prejudice in children.
ultiracial curriculum approach which emphasizes the diversity of racial
cultural beliefs and practices and gives them equal evaluation, may help
this process. Procedures such as Cooperative Group Work (Cowie &
dduck, 1991) bring children of different race (and sex) together
common activities, and may thus reduce ethnic preference and prejudice
the classroom.

INFLUENCES ON SOCIAL DEVELOPMENT: SUMMARY

he early important influences on the social development of the child are
clearly parents or caregivers. Through caregiver–infant interactions the
infant acquires basic social skills and develops social attachments.

As the child enters school and progresses to middle childhood, the
influence of peers becomes more important. Social participation and friendships with peers, and sociometric status in the peer group, appear to relate
in significant ways to later development. To some extent, the peer group is
an autonomous world with different systems, customs, and culture from the
adult world (Sluckin, 1981). Nevertheless, the family continues to exert an
influence, through patterns of attachment, management practices of parents
(including a direct influence on the out-of-school peer network), and the
effects of siblings. The older child, too, is increasingly aware of, and
influenced by, the expectations of society for someone of their age, gender,
ethnicity, and social background, as mediated by peers and by socializing
influences such as schools, and the mass media. By adolescence, the separation from parents is becoming more complete, and the young person is
moving toward a mature sense of identity and social being.

FURTHER READING

Aboud, F. (1988). *Children and prejudice*. Oxford: Basil Blackwell.
Bowlby, J. (1988). *A secure base: Clinical applications of attachment theory*.
London: Tavistock.
Dunn, J. (1988). *The beginnings of social understanding*. Oxford: Basil Blackwell.
Hargreaves, D., & Colley, A. (Eds) (1986). *The psychology of sex roles*. London:
Harper & Row.
McGurk, H. (Ed.) (1992). *Childhood social development: Contemporary perspect-
ives*. Hove: Lawrence Erlbaum.

REFERENCES

Aboud, F. (1988). *Children and prejudice*. Oxford: Basil Blackwell.

Table 2 Beliefs about boys and girls, held by both boys and girls aged $2\frac{1}{2}$ and $3\frac{1}{2}$[a]

Beliefs about girls	play with dolls
	like to help mother
	like to cook dinner
	like to clean house
	talk a lot
	never hit
	say "I need some help"
Beliefs about boys	like to help father
	say "I can hit you"

Source: Kuhn, Nash, and Bruken, 1978
Note: [a] Only results at or approaching statistical significance are recorded

By 8 years of age children's stereotypes are very similar to those obtained with adults.

EXPLANATIONS OF SEX DIFFERENCES

The sex differences in behaviour and sex-role stereotypes so far discussed apply to western urban societies such as the UK and the USA. Barry, Bacon, and Child (1957) made a survey of the anthropological literature on child-rearing in 110, mostly non-literate, societies. In more than 80 per cent of soci-eties, girls more than boys were encouraged to be nurturant, whereas boys more than girls were subject to training for self-reliance and achievement. In many societies responsibility and obedience were also encouraged in girls more than boys. Pressure for sex-typing is especially strong in societies where male strength is important for hunting or herding; it is less strong in societies with small family groups, where sharing of tasks is inevitable.

Sex hormones may have some effect on behaviour. In normal foetal development male sex hormones perhaps predispose boys to become more physically active and interested in rough-and-tumble play. This is consistent with evidence that such sex differences appear early in life, and in most human societies. However, biological factors do not in themselves explain the process of sex-role identification, and the variations in sex roles in different societies. Psychologists such as Bandura (1969) argue that children are moulded into sex-roles by the behaviour of adults, especially parents and teachers – the social learning theory approach. The idea of reinforcement is particularly important in this theory, which postulates that parents and others reward or "reinforce" sex-appropriate behaviour in children, for example encouraging nurturant behaviour in girls, and discouraging it in boys. Children may also observe the behaviour of same-sex models, and imitate them; for example, boys might observe and imitate the behaviour of male figures in TV films, in their playful and aggressive behaviour.

Kohlberg (1969) initiated a cognitive-developmental approach in this area, arguing that the child's growing sense of gender identity is crucial to sex-role identification. Children attend to and imitate same-sex models, and follow sex-appropriate activities, because they realize that this is what a child of their own sex usually does. This process has been termed "self-socialization" by Maccoby and Jacklin (1974), since it does not depend directly on external reinforcement. A number of studies have found development of gender identity and constancy to correlate with the degree of sex-typed behaviour.

While reinforcement does seem to have some effect, it looks as though its effects are being modulated by other factors. Any complete understanding of sex-role development will require an integration of biological factors, reinforcement, and social learning provided by others, with the cognitive-developmental view which provides an active role for the child himself or herself.

ETHNIC AWARENESS, IDENTITY, PREFERENCE, AND PREJUDICE

Besides differing by gender, people differ in terms of their racial or ethnic group; both are usually obvious from physical characteristics such as hair and skin colour, and facial appearance. There is not universal agreement on how people should be classified by ethnic group. Besides country of origin, other important dimensions are language (e.g., English Canadian and French Canadian) and religion (e.g., Muslim Indian and Hindu Indian).

As children grow up they will become aware that people differ by ethnic origin. By 4 or 5 years children seem able to make basic discriminations, for example between black and white; and during the next few years more difficult ones, such as Anglo and Hispanic. By around 8 or 9 years, children understand that ethnic identity remains constant despite changes in age, or superficial attributes such as clothing.

How do children react to, and evaluate, the ethnic differences which they become aware of from about 4 years? A number of studies of this kind have found that in a test situation where they can choose a doll, or photo, representing children of differing ethnicity, most white children choose or prefer the white doll (or photo) from 4 years, whereas black and other ethnic minority children are more divided, with (in some of the earlier studies) most of them choosing the white doll too. These preferences strengthen up to about 7 years. Beyond 7 years, black children tend to choose the black doll or photo more frequently. These studies were mostly carried out in North America or the UK, where whites form the dominant and more privileged social groups, and this probably influenced the results. The extent to which minority group children choose their own group has increased, at least

among 7 to 11 years old (Milner, 1983), with the rise of et consciousness and pride in their own culture which has c America and the UK since the 1970s.

Another way of looking at ethnic preference is more natu whom children actually choose as play partners, in playgrou situations. Children often segregate by race, as well as by ge and Haskins (1983) observed black and white kindergarten USA. They found that these 5 year olds showed marked segre which increased during a year in kindergarten. However, neit white children behaved differently towards other-colour peers they behaved towards same-colour peers.

In older children too, segregation by race is noticeable. Howev tion by race seems to be less marked than segregation by sex, by school period, and is not so evident among boys as girls, perha boys play in larger groups than girls; when playing football, for ethnic group may be ignored in order to fill up a team with the number of good players.

ETHNIC PREJUDICE

Preference is not identical with prejudice. Prejudice implies a negative ation of another person on the basis of some general attribute (which be for example sex, race, or disability). Thus, racial prejudice means a n ive evaluation of people as a consequence of their being in a certain ra or ethnic group. If a white child dislikes a black child because of some in vidual attribute, this is not prejudice. But if a white child dislikes a bla child (and black children) because of colour, this is racial prejudice. Th experience of prejudice can be very damaging and at times tragic. This i vividly brought to life in a case study at one school, *Murder in the Playground* (MacDonald, 1989).

Prejudice can be measured by asking children to put photos of other children from different ethnic groups along a scale of liking (Aboud, 1988), or to assign positive adjectives such as "work hard" and "truthful", or negative adjectives such as "stupid" or "dirty", to all, some, one or none of photos representing different ethnic groups (Davey, 1983). The results are rather similar to those of ethnic identity; prejudice seems to increase from 4 to 7 years, mainly at the expense of minority ethnic groups. During middle childhood, white children tend to remain prejudiced against black or minority group children, while the latter show a more mixed pattern but often become more positive to their own group.

Aboud (1988) has argued that before about 3 or 4 years of age, ethnic awareness is largely absent and prejudice is not an issue; but that from 4 to 7 years, children perceive other ethnic groups as dissimilar to themselves, and because of this tend to have negative evaluations of them. From 8 years

Ainsworth, M. D. S., Blehar, M. C., Waters, E., & Wall, S. (1978). *Patterns of attachment: A psychological study of the strange situation.* Hillsdale, NJ: Lawrence Erlbaum.

Bandura, A. (1969). Social learning theory of identificatory processes. In D. A. Goslin (Ed.) *Handbook of socialization theory and research* (pp. 213–262). Chicago, IL: Rand McNally.

Barry, H., III, Bacon, M. K., & Child, I. L. (1957). A cross-cultural survey of some sex differences in socialization. *Journal of Abnormal and Social Psychology, 55,* 327–332.

Belsky, J. (1988). Infant day care and socioemotional development: The United States. *Journal of Child Psychology and Psychiatry, 29,* 397–406.

Best, D. L., Williams, J. E., Cloud, L. M., Davis, S. W., Robertson, L. S., Edwards, J. R. Giles, H., & Fowles, J. (1977). Development of sex-trait stereotypes among young children in the United States, England and Ireland. *Child Development, 48,* 1375–1384.

Bigelow, B. J., & La Gaipa, J. J. (1980). The development of friendship values and choice. In H. C. Foot, A. J. Chapman, & J. R. Smith (Eds) *Friendship and social relations in children* (pp. 15–44). Chichester: Wiley.

Blurton Jones, N. (1967). An ethological study of some aspects of social behaviour of children in nursery school. In D. Morris (Ed.) *Primate ethology* (pp. 347–368). London: Weidenfeld & Nicolson.

Bowlby, J. (1953). *Child care and the growth of love.* Harmondsworth: Penguin.

Bowlby, J. (1969). *Attachment and loss: I. Attachment.* London: Hogarth.

Bretherton, I., & Waters, E. (Eds) (1985). Growing points of attachment theory and research. *Monographs of the Society for Research in Child Development, 50* (1–2).

Clark, A. H., Wyon, S. M., & Richards, M. P. M. (1969). Free-play in nursery school children. *Journal of Child Psychology and Psychiatry, 10,* 205–216.

Clarke-Stewart, A. (1989). Infant day care: Maligned or malignant? *American Psychologist, 44,* 266–273.

Cole, J. D., & Dodge, K. A. (1983). Continuities and changes in children's social status: A five-year longitudinal study. *Merrill-Palmer Quarterly, 29,* 261–282.

Costabile, A., Smith, P. K., Matheson, L., Aston, J., Hunter, T., & Boulton, M. (1991). Cross-national comparison of how children distinguish serious and playful fighting. *Developmental Psychology, 27,* 881–887.

Cowie, H., & Rudduck, J. (1991). *Cooperative group work in the multi-ethnic classroom.* London: BP.

Cummings, E. M., Iannotti, R. J., & Zahn-Waxler, C. (1989). Aggression between peers in early childhood: Individual continuity and developmental change. *Child Development, 60,* 887–895.

Davey, A. (1983). *Learning to be prejudiced: Growing up in multi-ethnic Britain.* London: Edward Arnold.

Dodge, K. A., Schlundt, D. C., Shocken, I., & Delugach, J. D. (1983). Social competence and children's sociometric status: The role of peer group entry strategies. *Merrill-Palmer Quarterly, 29,* 309–336.

Dodge, K. A., Pettit, G. S., McCluskey, C. L., & Brown, M. M. (1986). Social competence in children. *Monographs of the Society for Research in Child Development, 51,* 2.

Dunn, J., & Kendrick, C. (1982). *Siblings: Love, envy and understanding.* Oxford: Basil Blackwell.

Eibl-Eibesfeldt, I. (1989). *Human ethology.* New York: Aldine de Gruyter.

Falbo, T., & Polit, D. F. (1986). Quantitative review of the only child literature: Research evidence and theory development. *Psychological Bulletin, 100,* 176–189.

Farrington, D. P. (1991). Childhood aggression and adult violence: Early precursors and later-life outcomes. In D. J. Pepler & K. H. Rubin (Eds) *The development and treatment of childhood aggression* (pp. 5–29). Hillsdale, NJ: Lawrence Erlbaum.

Finkelstein, N. W., & Haskins, R. (1983). Kindergarten children prefer same-color peers. *Child Development, 54,* 502–508.

Furman, W., Rahe, D. F., & Hartup, W. W. (1979). Rehabilitation of socially withdrawn preschool children through mixed-age and same-age socialization. *Child Development, 50,* 915–922.

Hayvren, M., & Hymel, S. (1984). Ethical issues in sociometric testing: impact of sociometric measures on interaction behavior. *Developmental Psychology, 20,* 844–849.

Hertz-Lazarowitz, R., Feitelson, D., Zahavi, S., & Hartup, W. W. (1981). Social interaction and social organisation of Israeli five- to-seven-year olds. *International Journal of Behavioral Development, 4,* 143–155.

Jersild, A. T., & Markey, F. V. (1935). Conflicts between preschool children. *Child Development Monographs, 21.* Teachers College, Columbia University, New York.

Kaye, K. (1984). *The mental and social life of babies.* London: Methuen.

Kohlberg, L. (1969). Stages and sequence: The cognitive-developmental approach to socialization. In D. A. Goslin (Ed.) *Handbook of socialization theory and research* (pp. 347–480). Chicago, IL: Rand McNally.

Kuhn, D., Nash, S. C., & Bruken, L. (1978). Sex role concepts of two- and-three-year-olds. *Child Development, 49,* 445–451.

Ladd, G. W. (1983). Social networks of popular, averge and rejected children in school settings. *Merrill-Palmer Quarterly, 29,* 283–307.

Lever, J. (1978). Sex differences in the complexity of children's play and games. *American Sociological Review, 43,* 471–483.

Lewis, M., Young, G., Brooks, J., & Michalson, L. (1975). The beginning of friendship. In M. Lewis & L. Rosenblum (Eds) *Friendship and peer relations* (pp. 27–65). New York: Wiley.

Maccoby, E. E., & Jacklin, C. N. (1974). *The psychology of sex differences.* Stanford, CA: Stanford University Press.

MacDonald, I. (1989). *Murder in the playground.* London: Longsight.

Main, M. (1991). Metacognitive knowledge, metacognitive monitoring, and singular (coherent) vs. multiple (incoherent) model of attachment: Findings and directions for future research. In C. Murray Parkes, J. Stevenson-Hinde, & P. Marris (Eds) *Attachment across the life cycle* (pp. 127–159). London: Routledge.

Milner, D. (1983). *Children and race: Ten years on.* London: Ward Lock Educational.

Mueller, E., & Brenner, J. (1977). The origins of social skills and interaction among playgroup toddlers. *Child Development, 48,* 854–861.

O'Connor, R. D. (1972). Relative efficacy of modeling, shaping and the combined procedures for modification of social withdrawal. *Journal of Abnormal Psychology, 79,* 327–334.

Oden, S., & Asher, S. R. (1977). Coaching children in social skills for friendship making. *Child Development, 48,* 495–506.

Parker, J. G., & Asher, S. R. (1987). Peer relations and later personal adjustment: Are low-accepted children at risk? *Psychological Bulletin, 102,* 357–389.

Parten, M. B. (1932). Social participation among preschool children. *Journal of Abnormal and Social Psychology, 27,* 243–269.

Patterson, G. R., DeBaryshe, B. D., & Ramsey, E. (1989). A developmental perspective on antisocial behaviour. *American Psychologist, 44,* 329–335.

Sluckin, A. M. (1981). *Growing up in the playground: The social development of children,* London: Routledge & Kegan Paul.

Sluckin, A. M. & Smith, P. K. (1977). Two approaches to the concept of dominance in preschool children. *Child Development, 48,* 917–923.

Smith, P. K., & Thompson, D. A. (Eds) (1991). *Practical approaches to bullying.* London: David Fulton.

Trevarthen, C. (1977). Descriptive analyses of infant communicative behaviour. In H. R. Schaffer (Ed.) *Studies in mother–infant interaction* (pp. 227–270). London: Academic Press.

Turner, P. (1991). Relations between attachment, gender, and behavior with peers in preschool. *Child Development, 62,* 1475–1488.

Vaughn, B. E., & Langlois, J. H. (1983). Physical attractiveness as a correlate of peer status and social competence in preschool children. *Developmental Psychology, 19,* 561–567.

4

ADOLESCENCE

John C. Coleman

Trust for the Study of Adolescence, Brighton, England

Traditional theories	**Cognition**
Psychoanalytic theory	**Relationships with adults**
Sociological theory	**Conclusion**
The research evidence	**Further reading**
Puberty	**References**

In seeking to understand adolescence we are brought face to face with a variety of puzzling issues. In the first place no one is entirely sure when adolescence begins, and when it ends. It may be convenient to use the teenage years – from 13 to 19 – as one definition, but it hardly fits the facts. At one end puberty may commence at 10 or 11, and parents or teachers may describe the behaviour of girls or boys as "adolescent" well before they reach the age of 13. At the other end, those remaining in higher education, or still living at home in their early 20s, may be manifesting confrontational or dependent behaviour which is strikingly similar to that of a typical 14 year old.

We have only to consider current legislation to do with young people to see that age is a deeply confounding factor. Is adulthood reached at 16, 17, or at 18? Is a 10 year old a child or a young person? When do parental responsibilities cease? Asking such questions simply brings us face to face with the anomalies of the legal systems in many countries, anomalies that have a profound effect on young people themselves. The fact is that chronological age, although giving us a broad indication of the adolescent stage, cannot be a precise definition. Around the edges, and particularly at either end, the definition of adolescence remains uncertain, and this itself reflects an important feature of the phenomenon.

The second problem associated with adolescence has to do with the possibility that it is a stage that is to some extent artificially created. Many were influenced by Margaret Mead's classic book *Coming of Age in Samoa* (1928). In this book she describes a society in which individuals pass from childhood to adulthood with no trauma or stress. The existence of rites of passage enable boys and girls to be clear about when and how they should assume adult roles and responsibilities, and this clarity ensures that the long transition and the ambiguity of status are not experienced. Although it is generally agreed now that Mead viewed Samoan society through rose-coloured spectacles, none the less the sense continues to linger that western society, through its emphasis on continued education and the prolonged economic dependence of young people on their parents, encourages adolescence to be a difficult period.

Indeed, the teenage consumer has an important place in an industrial economy. The spending power of those who have as yet no adult responsibilities is formidable, and advertising and the media have devoted much of their energies to ensuring that this market not only remains in place, but also is expanded as far as possible. Such pressures undoubtedly play a part in creating younger and younger adolescents whose needs – for music, fashion, and so on – can be met only by new products.

However, this argument can be taken only so far. While it is certainly true that teenage consumers are an important element in western economies, that does not necessarily mean that our economic system – capitalism – has created adolescence. Adolescence has existed in one form or another since the Greeks, as we know from the writings of Plato. Two thousand years ago youth was seen as the political force most likely to challenge the status quo, and even in Elizabethan times, according to Shakespeare, the young were more likely to be "wronging the ancientry" and "getting wenches with child" than doing anything useful. A study by Montemayor (1983) analysed relationships between parents and adolescents in two historical periods – the 1920s and 1980s. He was able to show not only that issues of disagreement remained remarkably similar over the two periods, but, even more important, that levels of conflict within families were almost exactly the same. Clearly, therefore, in spite of enormous social and economic changes in the twentieth century, the phenomenon of adolescence has changed little. It is often said that the concept "the teenage years" came about after the end of the Second World War, and came to public notice in the 1950s with films such as James Dean's *Rebel without a Cause*. Montemayor's research shows this not to be true: it may be that the term "teenager" came into our vocabulary at that time, but adolescence itself has been around for very much longer. In fact the first substantial study of the psychology of adolescence was written by G. Stanley Hall; the date – 1904.

While adolescence is quite clearly affected by social and economic factors, and may manifest itself differently depending on the cultural and historical context, some form of transitional stage is common to most societies. The period of the transition will obviously vary both between and within societies. Thus, for example, in the United States and Britain work opportunities, housing, entry into further education, and family circumstances all affect the way adolescence shades into adulthood, and the length of time the transitional stage is allowed to continue.

Irrespective of when the stage ends, however, in most western countries there are particular characteristics of adolescence that are of general relevance. There seems little doubt, for example, that almost all young people experience ambiguity of status. Between the ages of 15 and 17 uncertainties about their rights, and lack of clarity about where they stand in relation to the authority of the parents, are issues familiar to many teenagers. "When do I become an adult?" is a tricky question to answer, and is likely to lead to confusion, not least because a different answer would be given by a police officer, a doctor, a teacher, a parent, and a social worker.

What is adolescence? It is a complex stage of human development, having some common features, but also involving enormously wide individual variations. In this chapter I shall be outlining some well-known theories of adolescence, as well as reviewing the results of some of the major research studies. I shall be concentrating on the common features of adolescence, but we should not lose sight of the fact that a stage which lasts for a minimum of six years cannot possibly be encapsulated in a few pages, and generalizations need to be treated with some care.

TRADITIONAL THEORIES

There is general agreement by all who have written about adolescence that it makes sense to describe the stage as being one of transition. The transition, it is believed, results from the operation of a number of pressures. Some of these, in particular the physiological and emotional pressures, are internal; while other pressures, which originate from peers, parents, teachers, and society at large, are external to the young person. Sometimes these external pressures carry the individual towards maturity at a faster rate than he or she would prefer, while on other occasions they act as a brake, holding the adolescent back from the freedom and independence which he or she believes to be a legitimate right. It is the interplay of these forces which, in the final analysis, contributes more than anything to the success or failure of the transition from childhood to maturity.

So far two classical types of explanation concerning the transitional process have been advanced. The psychoanalytic approach concentrates on the psychosexual development of the individual, and looks particularly at the psychological factors which underlie the young person's movement away from childhood behaviour and emotional involvement. The second type of explanation, the sociological, represents a very different perspective. While it has never been as coherently expressed as the psychoanalytic view, it is none the less of equal importance. In brief, this explanation sees the causes of adolescent transition as lying primarily in the social setting of the individual and concentrates on the nature of roles and role conflict, the pressures of social expectations, and on the relative influence of different agents of socialization. Let us now look more closely at each of these explanations.

Psychoanalytic theory

The psychoanalytic view of adolescence takes as its starting-point the upsurge of instincts which is said to occur as a result of puberty. This increase in instinctual life, it is suggested, upsets the psychic balance that has been achieved by the end of childhood causing internal emotional upheaval and leading to a greatly increased vulnerability of the personality. This state of affairs is associated with two further factors. In the first place, the individual's awakening sexuality leads him or her to look outside the family setting for appropriate "love objects" thus severing the emotional ties with the parents which have existed since infancy. This process is known as disengagement. Second, the vulnerability of the personality results in the employment of psychological defences to cope with the instincts and anxiety which are, to a greater or lesser extent, maladaptive. An excellent review of psychoanalytic thinking as it applies to adolescence may be found in Lerner (1987).

Regression, a manifestation of behaviour more appropriate to earlier stages of development, and ambivalence are both seen as further key elements of the adolescent process. According to the psychoanalytic view, ambivalence accounts for many of the phenomena often considered incomprehensible in adolescent behaviour. For example, the emotional instability of relationships, the contradictions in thought and feeling, and the apparently illogical shift from one reaction to another reflect the fluctuations between loving and hating, acceptance and rejection, involvement and noninvolvement which underlie relationships in the early years, and which are reactivated once more in adolescence.

Such fluctuations in mood and behaviour are indicative also of the young person's attitudes to growing up. Thus, while freedom may at times appear the most exciting of goals, there are also moments when, in the harsh light of reality, independence and the necessity to fight one's own battles become a daunting prospect. At these times childlike dependence exercises a powerful attraction, manifested in periods of uncertainty and self-doubt, and in behaviour that is more likely to bring to mind a wilful child than a young adult.

A consideration of ambivalence leads us on to the more general theme of non-conformity and rebellion, believed by psychoanalysts to be an almost universal feature of adolescence. Behaviour of this sort has many causes. Some of it is a direct result of ambivalent modes of relating, the overt reflection of the conflict between loving and hating. In other circumstances, however, it may be interpreted as an aid to the disengagement process. In this context if the parents can be seen as old-fashioned and irrelevant then the task of breaking the emotional ties becomes easier. If everything that originates from home can safely be rejected then there is nothing to be lost by giving it all up.

Non-conformity thus facilitates the process of disengagement although, as many writers point out, there are a number of intermediate stages along the way. Baittle and Offer (1971) illustrate particularly well the importance of non-conformity and its close links with ambivalence:

> When the adolescent rebels, he often expresses his intentions in a manner resembling negation. He defines what he does in terms of what his parents do not want him to do. If his parents want him to turn off the radio and study this is the precise time he keeps the radio on and claims he cannot study. If they want him to buy new clothes, "the old ones are good enough". In periods like this it becomes obvious that the adolescent's decisions are in reality based on the negative of the parents' wishes, rather than on their own positive desires. What they do and the judgements they make are in fact dependent on the parents' opinions and suggestions but in a negative way. This may be termed the stage of "negative dependence". Thus, while the oppositional behaviour and protest against the parents are indeed a manifestation of rebellion and in the service of emancipation from the parents, at the same time they reveal that the passive dependent longings are still in force. The adolescent is in conflict over desires to emancipate, and the rebellious behaviour is a compromise formation which supports his efforts to give up the parental object and, at the same time, gratifies his dependence on them. (p. 35)

To summarize, three particular ideas characterize the psychoanalytic position. In the first place adolescence is seen as being a period during which there is a marked vulnerability of personality, resulting primarily from the upsurge of instincts at puberty. Second, emphasis is laid on the likelihood of maladaptive behaviour, stemming from the inadequacy of the psychological defences to cope with inner conflicts and tensions. Examples of such behaviour include extreme fluctuations of mood, inconsistency in relationships, depression, and non-conformity. Third, the process of disengagement is given special prominence. This is perceived as a necessity if mature emotional and sexual relationships are to be established outside the home.

Sociological theory

As has been indicated, the sociological view of adolescence encompasses a very different perspective from that of psychoanalytic theory. While there is no disagreement between the two approaches concerning the importance of the transitional process, it is on the subject of the causes of this process that the viewpoints diverge. Thus, while the one concentrates on internal factors, the other looks at society and to events outside the individual for a satisfactory explanation. As will become apparent, it is implicit in the sociological viewpoint that both socialization and role assumption are more problematic during adolescence than at any other time.

Why should this be so? First, features of adolescence such as growing independence from authority figures, involvement with peer groups, and an unusual sensitivity to the evaluations of others all provoke role transitions and discontinuity, of varying intensities, as functions of both social and cultural context. Second, any inner change or uncertainty has the effect of increasing the individual's dependence on others, and this applies particularly to the need for reassurance and support for one's view of oneself. Third, the effects of major environmental changes are also relevant in this context. Different schools, the move from school to university or college, leaving home, taking a job, all demand involvement in a new set of relationships which in turn leads to different and often greater expectations, a substantial reassessment of the self, and an acceleration of the process of socialization. Role change, it will be apparent, is thus seen as an integral feature of adolescent development.

Socialization is seen as problematic for the following reasons. In the first place, the adolescent is exposed to a wide variety of competing socialization agencies, including the family, the school, the peer group, adult-directed youth organizations, the mass media, political organizations, and so on, and is thus presented with a wide range of potential conflicts, values, and ideals. Furthermore, it is commonly assumed by sociologists today that the socialization of young people is more dependent upon the generation than upon the family or other social institutions. Marsland (1987) goes so far as to call it "auto-socialization" in his description of the process:

> The crucial social meaning of youth is withdrawal from adult control and influence compared with childhood. Peer groups are the milieu into which young people withdraw. In at least most societies, this withdrawal to the peer group is, within limits, legitimated by the adult world. Time and space is handed over to young people to work out for themselves in auto-socialisation the developmental problems of self and identity which cannot be handled by the simple direct socialisation appropriate to childhood. There is a moratorium on compliance and commitment and leeway allowed for a relatively unguided journey with peers towards autonomy and maturity. (p. 12)

Both the conflict between socialization agencies and the freedom from clearly defined guidelines are seen as making socialisation more uncertain, and causing major difficulties for the young person in establishing a bridge towards the assumption of adult roles. Brake (1985), in his discussion of youth subcultures, makes similar points, and it is a common assumption among those writing from the sociological point of view that the social changes since the early 1970s have created ever-increasing stresses for young people.

To summarize, the sociological or social-psychological approach to adolescence is marked by a concern with roles and role change, and with the processes of socialization. There can be little doubt that adolescence, from this point of view, is seen as being dominated by stresses and tensions, not so much because of inner emotional instability, but as a result of conflicting pressures from outside. Thus, by considering both this and the psychoanalytic approach, two mutually complementary but essentially different views of the adolescent transitional process have been reviewed. In spite of their differences, however, the two approaches share one common belief, and that is in the concept of adolescent "storm and stress". Both these traditional theories view the teenage years as a "problem stage" in human development, and it is important therefore to see whether this view is borne out by the research evidence.

THE RESEARCH EVIDENCE

Broadly speaking, research provides little support for these traditional theories, and fails to substantiate much of what both psychoanalysts and sociologists appear to believe. To take some examples, while there is certainly some change in self-concept, there is no evidence to show that any but a small minority experience a serious identity crisis. In most cases, relationships with parents are positive and constructive, and young people do not in large part reject adult values in favour of those espoused by the peer group. In fact, in most situations peer-group values appear to be consistent with those of important adults rather than in conflict with them (Coleman & Hendry, 1990). Expectations of promiscuity among the young are not borne out by the research findings, nor do studies support the belief that the peer group encourages antisocial behaviour, unless other factors are also present. Lastly, there is no evidence to suggest that during the adolescent years there is a higher level of psychopathology than at other times. While a lot still needs to be learned about the mental health of young people, almost all the results that have become available so far indicate that, although a small minority may show disturbance, the great majority of teenagers seem to cope well and to show no undue signs of turmoil or stress.

Support for this belief may be found in every major study of adolescence that has appeared in recent years (Feldman & Elliott, 1990). Most would agree with the views of Siddique and D'Arcy (1984) who, in summarizing their own results on stress and well-being in adolescence, write as follows:

In this study some 33.5 per cent of the adolescents surveyed reported no symptoms of psychological distress, and another 39 per cent reported five or fewer symptoms (a mild level of distress). On the other hand a significant 27.5 per cent reported higher levels of psychological distress. For the majority the adolescent transition may be relatively smooth. However, for a minority it does indeed appear to be a period of stress and turmoil. The large majority of adolescents appear to get on well with adults and are able to cope effectively with demands of school and peer groups. They use their resources to make adjustments with environmental stressors with hardly visible signs of psychological distress. (p. 471)

There would appear to be a sharp divergence of opinion, therefore, between theory and research. Beliefs about adolescence that stem from traditional theory do not in general accord with the results of research. We need now to consider some of the reasons for this state of affairs. First, as many writers have pointed out, psychoanalysts and psychiatrists see a selected population. Their experience of adolescence is based primarily upon the individuals they meet in clinics or hospitals. Such experience is bound to encourage a somewhat one-sided perspective in which turmoil or disturbance is over-represented. For sociologists, on the other hand, the problem is often to disentangle concepts of "youth" or "the youth movement" from notions about young people themselves. As a number of commentators have observed, youth is frequently seen by sociologists as being in the forefront of social change. Youth is, as it were, the advance party where innovation or alteration in the values of society are concerned. From this position it is but a short step to use youth as a metaphor for social change, and thus to confuse radical forces in society with the beliefs of ordinary people (Brake, 1985).

Another possible reason for the divergence of viewpoint is that certain adolescent behaviours, such as vandalism, drug-taking, and hooliganism, are extremely threatening to adults. The few who are involved in such activities therefore attain undue prominence in the public eye. The mass media play an important part in this process by publicizing sensational behaviour, thus making it appear very much more common than it is in reality. One only has to consider critically the image of the teenager portrayed week after week on the television to understand how, for many adults, the minority comes to be representative of all young people. All three tendencies mentioned so far lead to an exaggerated view of the amount of turmoil that may be expected during adolescence, and thus serve to widen the gap between research and theory.

Obviously the two traditional theories have some value, and it would be wrong to leave the impression that neither is any longer relevant. Perhaps the most important contribution made by these theories is that they have provided the foundation for an understanding of young people with serious problems and a greater knowledge of those who belong to minority groups. In this respect the two major theories have much to offer. However, it must be recognized that they are now inadequate as the basis for an understanding of the development of the great majority of young people. The fact is that adolescence needs a theory, not of abnormality, but of normality. Any viable theoretical viewpoint put forward today must not only incorporate the results of empirical studies, but also acknowledge the fact that, although for some young people adolescence may be a difficult time, for the majority it is not a period of serious instability.

PUBERTY

Having considered theoretical approaches to adolescence, the rest of this chapter will be devoted to outlining three key areas of development —

puberty, cognition, and relationships with adults. Many other topics could have been included, but limitations of space have meant that selectivity has been inevitable. Puberty, and the physical growth that accompanies it, is important for a number of reasons. In the first place puberty has a range of physiological effects which are not always outwardly apparent to observers, but which can none the less have a considerable impact on the individual. Second, rates of maturation vary enormously leading inevitably to questions of normality and comparability between young people. Furthermore, especially early or unusually late developers have particular difficulties to face, which again have marked implications for classroom performance and behaviour. Third, physical development cannot fail to have psychological consequences, often affecting self-concept and self-esteem, factors which themselves play a major part in motivation and learning. Thus it can be seen that an understanding of puberty is essential in making sense of adolescent development as a whole.

Adults often fail to appreciate that puberty is accompanied by changes not only in the reproductive system and in the secondary sexual characteristics of the individual, but also in the functioning of the heart and thus of the cardiovascular system, in the lungs, which in turn affect the respiratory system, in the size and the strength of many of the muscles of the body, and so on. One of the many physical changes associated with puberty is the "growth spurt". This term is usually taken to refer to the accelerated rate of increase in height and weight that occurs during early adolescence. It is essential to bear in mind, however, that there are very considerable individual differences in the age of onset and duration of the growth spurt, even among perfectly normal children. This is a fact that parents and adolescents themselves frequently fail to appreciate, thus causing a great deal of unnecessary anxiety. In boys the growth spurt may begin as early as 10 years of age, or as late as 16, while in girls the same process can begin at 7 or 8, or not until 12, 13, or even 14. For the average boy, though, rapid growth begins at about 13, and reaches a peak somewhere between 14 and 15. Comparable ages for girls are 11 for the onset of the growth spurt and 12 for the peak age of increase in height and weight. Other phenomena associated with the growth spurt are a rapid increase in the size and weight of the heart (the weight of the heart nearly doubles at puberty), accelerated growth of the lungs, and a decline in basal metabolism. Noticeable to children themselves, especially boys, is a marked increase in physical strength and endurance (see Tanner, 1978, for a full description).

Sexual maturation is closely linked with the physical changes described above. Again, the sequence of events is approximately 18 to 24 months later for boys than it is for girls. Since individuals mature at very different rates, one girl at the age of 14 may be small, have no bust, and look very much as she did during childhood, while another of the same age may look like a fully developed adult woman, who could easily be taken for someone four or five years in advance of her actual chronological age.

The changes discussed above inevitably exercise a profound effect upon the individual. The body alters radically in size and shape, and it is not surprising that many adolescents experience a period of clumsiness in an attempt to adapt to these changes. The body also alters in function, and new and sometimes worrying physical experiences, such as the girl's first menstrual period, have to be understood. Perhaps most important of all, however, is the effect that such physical changes have upon identity. As many writers have pointed out, the development of the individual's identity requires not only the notion of being separate and different from others, but also a sense of self-consistency, and a firm knowledge of how one appears to the rest of the world. Needless to say, dramatic bodily changes seriously affect these aspects of identity, and represent a considerable challenge in adaptation for even the most well-adjusted young person. It is unfortunate that many adults, having successfully forgotten much of their own adolescent anxiety, retain only a vague awareness of the psychological impact of the physical changes associated with puberty.

COGNITION

In a short review such as this it is possible only to draw attention to the major themes, and to highlight one or two of the most significant areas of work in this field. For those wishing to read further, good general discussions of cognition in adolescence are to be found in Coleman and Hendry (1990), Serafica (1982), and Conger and Petersen (1984). Changes in intellectual functioning during the teenage years have implications for a wide range of behaviours and attitudes. Such changes render possible the move towards independence of both thought and action; they enable the young person to develop a time perspective that includes the future; they facilitate progress towards maturity in relationships; and finally they underline the individual's ability to participate in society as worker, voter, responsible group member, and so on. We cannot consider these changes without looking first at the work of Piaget, for it is he who has laid the foundation for almost all subsequent work on cognitive development. It will be worthwhile also to discuss briefly some work on adolescent reasoning and to review ideas on both moral and political thought in adolescence.

The work of Jean Piaget, the Swiss psychologist, is the most obvious starting-point for a consideration of cognitive development during the adolescent years. It was he who first pointed out that a qualitative change in the nature of mental ability, rather than any simple increase in cognitive skills, is to be expected at or around puberty, and he has argued that it is at this point in development that formal operational thought becomes possible (Inhelder & Piaget, 1958). A full description of Piaget's stages of cognitive growth is not possible here. According to Piaget, in early adolescence the individual moves from a stage of concrete operations to one of formal operational thought. With the appearance of this stage a number of capabilities become available to the young person. Perhaps the most significant of these is the ability to construct "contrary to fact" propositions. This change has been described as the shift of emphasis in adolescent thought from the "real" to the "possible", and it facilitates hypothetico-deductive logic. It also enables the individual to think about mental constructs as objects that can be manipulated, and to come to terms with notions of probability and belief.

This fundamental difference in approach between the young child and the adolescent has been neatly demonstrated in a study by Elkind (1966). He showed dramatic differences between 8 and 9 year olds and 13 and 14 year olds in their capacity to solve a concept-formation problem by setting up hypotheses and then testing them out in logical succession. However, it is clear that formal operational thought cannot be tested using a single problem task. Any investigator must use a range of tests in an attempt to construct some overall measure of the individual's ability to tackle problems of logical thought in a number of areas. In relation to this it is important to bear in mind that the development of formal thinking is certainly not an all-or-nothing affair, with the individual moving overnight from one stage to another. The change occurs slowly, and there may even be some shifting back and forth before the new mode of thought is firmly established. Furthermore, it is almost certain that the adolescent will adopt formal modes of thinking in one area before another. Thus, for example, someone interested in arts subjects may use formal operational thinking in the area of verbal reasoning well before he or she is able to utilize such skills in scientific problem solving.

In addition to these points, research has indicated that in all probability Piaget was a little too optimistic when he expressed the view that the majority of adolescents could be expected to develop formal operational thought by 12 or 13 years of age. While studies do not entirely agree on the exact proportions reaching various stages at different age levels, there is general consensus that up to the age of 16 only a minority reach the most advanced level of formal thought (Coleman & Hendry, 1990).

One area of particular interest to researchers in the field of cognitive development is that of moral and political thought. How is this changed by formal operations? Do young people pass through different stages of thinking where morals and politics are concerned, and if so, what is the nature of such stages? As far as moral thinking is concerned it is once again Piaget's notions which have formed the springboard for later thinking on this subject, enabling Kohlberg to develop his "cognitive-developmental" approach.

Kohlberg (1969) elaborated Piaget's early ideas into a scheme that has six different stages. His method was to present hypothetical situations concerning moral dilemmas to young people of different ages, and to classify their responses according to a stage theory of moral development. Some of Kohlberg's most interesting work involved the study of moral development in different cultures. He showed that an almost identical sequence appears to occur in widely different cultures, the variation between cultures being found in the rate of development, and the fact that in more primitive societies later stages of thinking are rarely used.

As in the case of moral judgement, the young person's political ideas are likely to be significantly influenced by his or her level of cognitive development. Since the 1960s a number of writers have become interested in the shift that takes place during the adolescent years, from a lack of political thought to – in many cases – an intense involvement in this area of life. How does this occur and what are the processes involved? At what age do adolescents begin to show an increasing grasp of political concepts, and what stages do they go through before they achieve maturity of political judgement? One of the most important early studies was that undertaken by Adelson and O'Neill (1966). They approached the problem of the growth of political ideas in an imaginative way by posing for young people of different ages the following problem: "Imagine that a thousand men and women, dissatisfied with the way things are going in their own country, decide to purchase and move to an island in the Pacific; once there they must devise laws and codes of government". They then explored the adolescents' approach to a variety of relevant issues. They asked questions about how a government would be formed, what would its purpose be, would there be a need for laws and political parties, how would you protect minorities, and so on. The investigators proposed different laws, and explored typical problems of public policy.

The major results may be discussed under two headings – the changes in modes of thinking, and the decline of authoritarianism with age. As far as the first is concerned, there was a marked shift in thinking from the concrete to the abstract, a finding which ties in well with the work discussed above. The second major shift observed was the decline in authoritarian solutions to political questions. The typical young adolescent appeared unable to appreciate that problems can have more than one solution, and that individual behaviour or political acts are not necessarily absolutely right or wrong, good or bad. The concept of moral relativism was not yet available for the making of political judgements. In contrast, the 14 or 15 year old is much more aware of the different sides of any argument, and is usually able to take a relativistic point of view. Thinking begins to be more tentative, more critical and more pragmatic.

Work in this area has been well reviewed by Furnham and Stacey (1991). As they indicate, we now know a lot more about the ways in which thinking in the political arena develops. It is a topic of particular interest, not only because of its obvious implications for education and government, but also because of the manner in which intellectual change can be seen to interact with social behaviour. This is not to say that other areas of cognitive development are not of equal value and importance, and it is to be hoped that this chapter may act as a signpost, if nothing more, towards issues of general interest.

RELATIONSHIPS WITH ADULTS

One of the central themes of adolescent development is the attainment of independence, often represented symbolically in art and literature by the moment of departure from home. However, for most young people independence is not gained at one specific moment by the grand gesture of saying goodbye to one's parents and setting off to seek one's fortune in the wide world. Independence is much more likely to mean the freedom to make new relationships, and personal freedom to take responsibility for oneself in such things as education, work, political beliefs, and future career choice.

Many forces interact in propelling an individual towards a state of maturity. Naturally both physical and intellectual maturation encourage the adolescent towards greater autonomy. In addition to these factors there are, undoubtedly, psychological forces within the individual as well as social forces within the environment that have the same goal. In the psychoanalytic view, mentioned earlier, the process of seeking independence represents the need to break off the infantile ties with the parents, thus making new mature sexual relationships possible. From the perspective of the sociologist, more emphasis is placed on the changes in role and status which lead to a redefinition of the individual's place in the social structure. Whatever the explanation, it is certainly true that the achievement of independence is an integral feature of adolescent development, and that the role of the adults involved is an especially important one.

In understanding this process it is necessary to appreciate that the young person's movement towards adulthood is far from straightforward. While independence at times appears to be a rewarding goal, there are moments when it is a worrying, even frightening, prospect. Childlike dependence can be safe and comforting at no matter what age, if, for example, one is facing problems or difficulties alone, and it is essential to realize that no individual achieves adult independence without a number of backward glances. It is this ambivalence that underlies the typically contradictory behaviour of adolescence, behaviour that is so often the despair of adults. Thus there is nothing more frustrating than having to deal with a teenager who is at one moment complaining about adults who are always interfering, and the next bitterly protesting that no one takes any interest. However, it is equally important to acknowledge that adults themselves usually hold conflicting attitudes towards young people. On the one hand they may wish them to be independent, to make their own decisions, and to cease making childish demands, while on the other they may be anxious about the consequences of independence, and sometimes jealous of the opportunities and idealism of youth. In addition it should not be forgotten that the adolescent years often coincide with the difficulties of middle age for parents in particular. Adjusting to unfulfilled hopes, the possibility of retirement, declining physical health, marital difficulties, and so on may all increase family stress, and add further to the problems faced by young people in finding a satisfactory route to independence.

Research evidence has not provided much support for the notion that wide-ranging conflict between adults and young people is the order of the day. Noller and Callan (1991), in reviewing the data available, come to the conclusion that the general picture that emerges from experimental studies is one of relatively harmonious relationships with adults for the majority of young people. Of course adolescents do seek independence, of that there is no dispute, and so the question arises as to how common sense and research evidence can be fitted together. In the first place it is clear that some adolescents do, temporarily at least, come into conflict with or become critical of adults. In addition there is no doubt that some adults do become restrictive, attempting to slow down the pace of change. Research has shown that there are a number of factors that affect the extent of the conflict occurring between the generations. Cultural background, adult behaviour, age, and social class all need to be taken into account.

Other aspects of the situation need also to be borne in mind. For example, there is undoubtedly a difference between attitudes towards close family members, and attitudes to more general social groupings, such as "the younger generation". Thus, for example, teenagers may very well approve of and look up to their own parents while expressing criticism of adults in general. Similarly, parents may deride "drop-outs", "skinheads", or "soccer hooligans" while holding a favourable view of their own adolescent sons and daughters. Another fact that needs to be stressed is that there is a difference between feeling and behaviour. Adolescents may be irritated or angry with their parents as a result of day-to-day conflicts, but issues can be worked out in the home, and do not necessarily lead to outright rejection or rebellion. Furthermore, too little credit is given to the possibility that adults and young people, although disagreeing with each other about certain things, may still respect each other's views, and live or work together in relative harmony. Thus there seems to be little doubt that the extreme view of a generation gap, involving the notion of a war between the generations, or the ideas of a separate adolescent subculture, is dependent on a myth. It is the result of a stereotype which is useful to the mass media, and given currency by a small minority of disaffected young people and resentful adults. However, to deny any sort of conflict between teenagers and older members of society is equally false. Adolescents could not grow into adults unless they were able to test out the boundaries of authority, nor could they discover what they believed unless given the opportunity to push hard against the beliefs of others. The adolescent transition from dependence to independence is almost certain to involve some conflict, but its extent should not be exaggerated.

CONCLUSION

Adolescence is, to many, a confusing concept. Its definition is uncertain, its characteristics contradictory, and much behaviour associated with this stage in development is difficult to understand. Classical theories of adolescence – those originating from psychoanalysis and sociology – have been helpful in unravelling some of the more extreme types of behaviour and, in the case of psychoanalysis, contributing to developments in the treatment of disturbance. None the less, empirical evidence shows wide individual variation in the abilities of young people to adjust to the transition from childhood to adulthood.

Many factors, such as family context, maturational timing, educational ability, and so on, will contribute to the adolescent's capacity to cope with the social and emotional changes inevitable during the teenage years. However, based on the research that has appeared in many different countries since the 1960s, it appears to be the case that the majority of young people, in western countries at least, do not suffer a major identity crisis, nor do they experience a serious breakdown in relationships within the family. While all will have conflicts and pressures to deal with, most appear to do so without excessive trauma.

As I have indicated, there is wide individual variation in adjustment, and in considering adolescence, and the factors that contribute to young people's experience of growing up, two important dimensions need to be kept in mind. First, the social circumstances of childhood and adolescence cannot be ignored. As one example of this, since the early 1980s we have become more aware of the impact of poverty, and its devastating consequences on the occupational and family careers of young people. Second, culture too plays a major role in facilitating or hindering individuals' opportunities to make the full use of their potential. Questions of ethnic identity, widely differing attitudes to the roles of boys and girls in the family, living through racial prejudice or harassment – such things may loom very large indeed in the lives of individual adolescents.

Adolescence is an important transitional stage in human development. If we wish to understand it, however, we need to remember that no generalizations, even in relation to one culture, one country, one location even, will do justice to the complexity of the adolescent experience. Theory and research have taken us a long way forward since Hall's publication of 1904, but we still have much to learn before we can fully grasp the complexity of the second decade of life.

FURTHER READING

Coleman, J. C., & Hendry, L. (1990). *The nature of adolescence* (2nd edn). London and New York: Routledge.
Feldman, S. S., & Elliott, G. (1990). *At the threshold: The developing adolescent.* London: Harvard University Press.
Kroger, J. (1989). *Identity in adolescence: The balance between self and other.* London: Routledge.
Noller, P., & Callan, V. (1991). *The adolescent in the family.* London: Routledge.

REFERENCES

Adelson, J., & O'Neill, R. (1966). The development of political thought in adolescence. *Journal of Personality and Social Psychology, 4,* 295–308.
Baittle, B., & Offer, D. (1971). On the nature of adolescent rebellion. In F. C. Feinstein, P. Giovacchini, & A. Miller (Eds) *Annals of adolescent psychiatry* (pp. 22–57). New York: Basic Books.
Brake, M. (1985). *Comparative youth subcultures.* London: Routledge & Kegan Paul.
Coleman, J. C., & Hendry, L. (1990). *The nature of adolescence* (2nd edn). London and New York: Routledge.
Conger, J., & Petersen, A. (1984). *Adolescence and youth* (3rd edn). New York: Harper & Row.
Elkind, D. (1966). Conceptual orientation shifts in children and adolescents. *Child Development, 37,* 493–498.
Elkind, D. (1967). Egocentrism in adolescence. *Child Development, 38,* 1025–1034.
Feldman, S. S., & Elliott, G. (1990). *At the threshold: The developing adolescent.* London: Harvard University Press.
Furnham, A., & Stacey, B. (1991). *Young people's understanding of society.* London: Routledge.
Hall, G. C. (1904). *Adolescence.* New York: Appleton.
Inhelder, B., & Piaget, J. (1958). *The growth of logical thinking.* London: Routledge & Kegan Paul.
Kohlberg, L. (1969). *Stages in development of moral thought and action.* New York: Holt, Rinehart & Winston.
Lerner, R. M. (1987). Psychodynamic models. In V. B. Van Hasselt & M. Hersen (Eds) *Handbook of adolescent psychology* (pp. 53–76). Oxford: Pergamon.
Marsland, D. (1987). *Education and youth.* London: Falmer.
Mead, M. (1928). *Coming of age in samoa.* New York: Morrow.
Montemayor, R. (1983). Parents and adolescents in conflict: All families some of the time and some families most of the time. *Journal of Early Adolescence, 3,* 83–103.
Noller, P., & Callan, V. (1991). *The adolescent in the family.* London: Routledge.
Serafica, F. C. (Ed.) (1982). *Social-cognitive development in context.* London: Methuen.
Siddique, C. M., & D'Arcy, C. (1984). Adolescence, stress and psychological well-being. *Journal of Youth and Adolescence, 13,* 459–474.
Tanner, J. M. (1978). *Foetus into man.* London: Open Books.

AGEING

John C. Cavanaugh
University of Delaware, USA

Roughly a century ago, Oliver Wendell Holmes, a member of the United States Supreme Court and a poet, wrote that "to be 70 years young is sometimes far more cheerful and hopeful than to be 40 years old". Holmes's use of "young" to describe a 70 year old and "old" to describe a 40 year old is far more than a literary device. It is possible that he was trying to make the same point as late twentieth-century psychologists: growing old is as much,

Reaction time

reds of studies point to a clear conclusion: people slow (Salthouse, 1985). Indeed, the slowing-with-age phenom- ocumented that many gerontologists accept it as the only ural change yet discovered. Evidence to back up this claim eral sources, including simple, choice, and complex reaction lthouse, 1985). Two aspects of the actual response made in tasks appear to change with age. First, older adults do not pre- ond as well as younger adults. Second, the complexity of the ferentially affects older adults; the more complex the response, lder adults are slowed relative to younger adults.

nterventions help older adults perform better on reaction time st, practice with making rapid responses improves older adults' per- e, but usually does not close the age gap completely. Second, using rld tasks can help as well. Salthouse (1984) reported age differences ndard reaction time tasks but no age differences on a typing task, due e fact that typists had learned to compensate for slower reaction times eing able to anticipate upcoming letters. Finally, people who engage in tained aerobic exercise have better reaction time performance relative to dentary people (Baylor & Spirduso, 1988).

MEMORY

More research has been conducted on memory than on any other topic in cognitive ageing. Our survey of this large literature will focus on several topics of current interest: working memory, secondary memory, storage and retrieval processes, prose, everyday memory, self-evaluation, clinical issues, and remediation.

Working memory

Working memory is a small-capacity store that deals with items currently being processed. There is growing evidence that the capacity of working memory declines somewhat with age (Salthouse, 1991), with the result being poorer quality information being passed along the system. The difficulty appears to involve how efficiently working memory operates. For example, older adults show a loss of efficiency in working memory with age even with substantial practice on a mental arithmetic task. Because changes in efficiency may potentially affect many other aspects of information-processing, some researchers (Salthouse, 1991) argue that age-related changes in working memory may underlie cognitive changes in general.

if not more, a state of mind that a state of inevitable playing out of some genetic programme.

The inclusion of a chapter on ageing in this volume is recognition of a profound revolution: the restructuring of the world's population from one that is dominated by youth to one that now includes many older people as well. This revolution has changed the way people experience daily life (e.g., death is now viewed as the province of the old in industrialized nations) and each other (e.g., knowing one's great-grandparents is now common), as well as how governments interact with citizens (e.g., the need to develop programmes for long-term care). All of this has happened without fanfare and in spite of world wars and numerous natural disasters.

This chapter is about understanding the revolutionaries, elderly people in modern society. Clearly, our overview must be selective. Thus, we shall consider a few areas of cognitive development (attention, reaction time, memory, and intelligence), personality, depression and dementia, retirement, grandparenting, and widowhood. Readers desiring more complete coverage have many options at both the introductory level and the professional level, as noted below under "Further Reading".

THE CONTEXTS OF AGEING

In order to understand the ageing process, it is necessary to use a multidisciplinary framework that includes various influences on development. The biopsychosocial model provides a context for considering influences in three major arenas: biological, psychological, and social. This model highlights the fact that ageing is not the result of any one of these influences alone; rather, all three must be considered together. The biopsychosocial model consists of four main components, each of which focuses on a different set of issues: interpersonal factors, intrapersonal factors, biological and physical factors, and life cycle factors. We shall consider each of these factors briefly.

Interpersonal factors include all of the various aspects of social support an individual has in his or her present situation. For example, the degree to which someone has a collaborative relationship with family and friends and the interpersonal skills one has for dealing with interpersonal relationships are aspects of interpersonal factors. In general, these factors describe the social milieu in which an individual exists.

Intrapersonal factors reflect personal characteristics such as age, gender, genetic inheritance, and physiological systems such as the central nervous system. In addition, intrapersonal factors include psychological characteristics such as personality, intelligence, sensory-perceptual functioning, and motor functioning. In short, intrapersonal factors involve all of the aspects of a normal functioning individual.

Biological and physical factors represent degenerative influences of chronic illness, functional incapacities, and physical diseases (such as cardiovascular diseases, cancer, and the like). These factors reflect processes that ultimately lead to death. These disease factors play a very important role in understanding ageing, as many of them are associated with negative images of ageing. For example, many people erroneously believe that most older people get Alzheimer's disease. (In fact, the incidence is roughly 10 per cent of people over age 65.) Because biological and physical factors represent decline, they play a major role in setting the overall context of ageing.

Life cycle factors include four distinct things: past social experiences (e.g., accomplishments, adversities, stressful events, economic changes); past physical experiences (e.g., acute diseases, psychobiological predispositions to disease, psychological disorders); current functioning (e.g., current hopes, motivation, attitudes towards ageing); and future perspectives (e.g., anxieties, hopes, and dreams about what life will be like). Life cycle factors help place people in a specific historical time in relation to their own lifespan and sociocultural history.

Most of the research reviewed in this chapter pertains to intrapersonal factors. That is, the emphasis is on normal individual development across adulthood. However, we shall consider a few topics represented by the remaining factors (e.g., Alzheimer's disease).

ATTENTION AND REACTION TIME

The information-processing model has been adopted by researchers in cognitive ageing as a general framework in which to study how people deal with incoming stimuli and how these processes change over time. Some age differences have been noted in some of the early aspects of information-processing, such as decreases in encoding speed and increased susceptibility to backward masking (Kline & Schieber, 1985). Unfortunately, little research has been conducted on these early steps in information-processing; consequently, we do not know how these age differences affect later phases. Much clearer, though, are age differences in attention and reaction time.

Attention

Although everyone has some intuitive understanding of what attention is, it turns out to be rather difficult to define precisely. About the best researchers can do is describe three interdependent aspects of it: selectivity (referring to the limited ability to process information), capacity (referring to how much information can be processed), and vigilance (referring to how long we are able to maintain focused attention).

Selectivity

Several different aspects of age differences in attentional selectivity have

been studied. The evidence indic... than younger adults visually ... (Plude & Hoyer, 1985). I... equally able to extract inf... ically, older adults have mo... about the target together. Wh... a target, older adults have mor... appears that provides unambiguou... will be (Plude & Doussard-Roosve... older adults are sometimes as able to sv... adults on visual tasks (Hartley & McKen... are able to switch from a narrow focus (suc... letter word) to a broad focus (such as all fiv...

The most prominent age differences in atten... the task. For example, McDowd, Filion, and O... that when relevant and irrelevant information are b... modality (such as visually), older adults distribute... equally between the two types of information than... However, when relevant information was presented in ... visually) and irrelevant information in another (say, auditor... younger adults show similar patterns of attention allocation.

Capacity

How much information adults can process at the same time is typical... amined in divided attention tasks, in which people are asked to perform ... tasks at once. Age differences emerge as a function of task complexity. Whe... divided attention tasks are relatively easy, age differences are typically absent. However, when the tasks become more complicated, age differences favouring younger adults are found (McDowd & Craik, 1988).

Vigilance

Little research has been done examining age differences in how long people can maintain attention. What little there is suggests that older adults are not as accurate as younger adults at identifying targets correctly, but no age differences appear in the rate at which performance declines over time. Specifically, it appears that older adults are not as alert as younger adults while performing vigilance tasks. Moreover, older adults' performance does not improve to the level of younger adults' performance even after considerably longer training periods (Fisk & Rogers, 1987).

Secondary memory

Secondary memory involves the ability to remember rather extensive amounts of information over relatively long periods. Typically, secondary memory is studied through recall and recognition paradigms involving the retention of many different types of material. The results from hundreds of studies point to several conclusions. Older adults tend to perform worse than younger adults on recall tests, but these differences are less apparent or may be eliminated on recognition tests (Poon, 1985). Older adults tend to be less efficient at spontaneously using strategies, such as putting items into categories, during study. When instructed to do so, however, older adults not only do so, but show improved performance as well. Overall, these data show that older adults are not as good as younger adults at devising ways to learn and remember information on their own, but are able to benefit to some degree from cues during learning and retrieval. Age differences can be reduced in several ways, such as slowing down the rate of presentation of information, allowing older adults to practise the task, and by using familiar information.

Storage and retrieval processes

The age differences in performance on secondary memory tasks imply age differences in the underlying processes of storage and retrieval. The available evidence suggests that: first, changes in memory with ageing are a result of decrements in both storage and retrieval; second, these decrements are more substantial for retrieval; and third, these decrements occur in specific sub-components of storage and retrieval and do not generalize to all of them (Howe, 1988). For example, older adults are less likely to use connections between incoming words and words they already know to help remember the stimuli, but, once the connections are made, older adults remember them as well as younger adults (Howe, 1988). Moreover, older and younger adults are equally good at using generic retrieval strategies, but younger adults are better at using specialized retrieval strategies (Howe, 1988).

Prose memory

How well adults remember the material they read is a rapidly-growing area in memory research. Whether one finds age differences in prose memory depends on several things. In general, age differences in remembering prose are minimised when tasks are made more naturalistic by providing unlimited study time, using long text passages, and requiring only a general summary rather than details. Several other factors are also important. Adults with little education and who have low verbal ability tend to do much worse on prose memory tasks than other groups (Meyer, 1987). How much people know about the topic they are reading also matters; high prior knowledge is usually an asset. Rapid presentation of reading material tends to differentially penalize older adults. Finally, when text material is clearly organized, with emphasis on structure and the main ideas, older and younger adults perform equivalently in distinguishing between the main ideas and the details.

Everyday memory

Despite the large number of studies investigating age differences in memory, little is known about how memory performance changes in everyday life. This is largely because the tasks used in most research on memory ageing involve list learning. In everyday life, many other tasks are faced, such as remembering where something is located or what actions were performed earlier. Due to the concern about the potential lack of generalizability of list learning to everyday life, several researchers began investigating memory in other tasks.

Results from several studies of memory for location indicate that older adults perform better in familiar settings and use different search strategies than younger adults. Actually performing actions (rather than merely watching them) helps older adults remember activities (Cohen & Faulkner, 1989). However, older adults are more likely to claim that they remember performing actions that they in fact only observed (Cohen & Faulkner, 1989). Several researchers (e.g., Poon & Schaffer, 1982) have shown that older adults are consistently superior to younger adults in remembering to remember (e.g., remembering to mail a postcard on a certain day).

Self-evaluation

Because memory is used by many older adults as a means of judging their overall cognitive competence, it is important to establish whether the evaluations they make are a reflection of accurate information. Research on the processes underlying memory self-evaluations examines this issue. Older adults tend to rate their memory as poorer than younger adults rate theirs. It appears that older adults know less about the internal workings of memory and its capacity, view memory as less stable, expect that memory will deteriorate with age, and perceive that they have less control over memory (Dixon & Hultsch, 1983). Older adults report that remembering names is especially troublesome, but report no more problems remembering appointments and errands than do younger adults (Cavanaugh, Grady, & Perlmutter, 1983).

If asked to predict how well they will do on a task they have not seen, older adults tend to overestimate their performance while younger adults tend to be more accurate. However, if they are allowed to see or practise the task first, older adults are just as accurate as younger adults in predicting their performance.

Clinical issues

The large research literature on age differences in memory have helped establish guidelines for distinguishing between normal and abnormal ageing. In general, normative age-related decrements in memory do not significantly interfere with daily life. If such interference is observed, then the changes may not be normative and should be investigated further. Whether such changes indicate a serious pathology such as dementia depends, however. Many physical and mental disorders may affect memory performance, including depression, certain nutritional deficiencies, and several types of medications. If abnormal memory changes are suspected, a full diagnostic work-up should include a complete physical examination, blood tests, neurological screening, and neuropsychological tests.

Remediation

If a memory impairment has been identified, or if an older person simply desires to compensate for normative changes, several types of remediation approaches are available. First, memory strategies may be trained. Yesavage (1983) has developed a successful programme to train older adults to use imagery strategies to help themselves remember names. Similar training programmes have been developed for retrieval strategies. For example, Camp and McKitrick (1991) report the successful application of a spaced retrieval strategy to persons with Alzheimer's disease to help them learn the names of staff members. Second, memory exercises such as rehearsing a grocery list over and over appear to work as well. Third, the most popular approach has been the use of external strategies, such as making lists and keeping appointment calendars (Cavanaugh et al., 1983).

INTELLIGENCE

Research on the development of general intellectual skills has followed two main research traditions: the psychometric tradition and the cognitive-process tradition. The psychometric tradition includes all the standardized intelligence tests, and emphasizes how many items are answered correctly in each of several domains. In contrast, the cognitive-process approach stresses the qualitative nature of intelligence by emphasising the thought processes underlying the response rather than its accuracy. Each approach paints a different picture of intellectual development across adulthood.

Psychometric approach

The psychometric approach is based on the notion that related intellectual skills are hierarchically organized into an overall structure of intelligence. To date, researchers have identified numerous intellectual abilities at two different levels in the hierarchy. First, the primary mental abilities are those that are tapped by various intelligence tests. Second, the primary mental abilities are themselves organized into secondary mental abilities.

In a complex longitudinal study begun in 1956, Schaie tests seven cohorts of people every seven years. Based on two separate sets of fourteen-year longitudinal data, Schaie and Hertzog (1983) demonstrated age changes on five primary mental abilities: number, work fluency, verbal meaning, inductive reasoning, and spatial ability. The magnitude of the decline in individuals between age 50 and 60 was minimal. However, the changes in people over age 60 was large enough for individuals to notice the difference in everyday life.

Relationships among the various mental abilities tapped directly by intelligence tests have been studied as well. Two of these higher-order abilities that have received the most attention are fluid and crystallized intelligence. Fluid intelligence refers to innate abilities that are not the product of experience or education, but are thought to provide the basis for learning. Typically, research findings show that fluid intelligence declines across adulthood (Horn, 1982). In contrast, crystallized intelligence is the result of experience and education, and typically shows stability or improvement across adulthood (Horn, 1982).

In an attempt to explain the different developmental patterns of fluid and crystallized intelligence, researchers have identified several important variables. One of the most important is cohort effects, which relate to differences in key experiences as a function of when people were born (Labouvie-Vief, 1985). For example, individuals born in the 1930s did not have computers as part of their educational experience like those born in the 1970s did. Such differences become reflected in how and what people learn, which in turn affects their scores on intelligence tests. Additionally, educational level, occupation, personality, health, and the relevance of test materials have also been shown to explain part of the age changes (Labouvie-Vief, 1985). Nevertheless, even when moderators are taken into account, age differences between younger and older adults are never completely eliminated (Schaie & Hertzog, 1983).

The normative declines in fluid intelligence have led some authors to speculate whether such changes are simply inevitable or are due to lack of practice. That is, it is possible that declines in fluid abilities reflect changes in cognitive demands placed on adults, and not an inevitable part of the ageing process. Baltes and Willis (1982) initiated a series of studies called Project ADEPT examining this issue by training adults on primary mental abilities that show decline over time. Baltes and Willis demonstrated that people's performance on these abilities improved significantly after training, supporting the view that the observed declines may not be inevitable and irreversible.

Subsequently, other researchers have confirmed Baltes and Willis's (1982) results. Some have shown that direct training may not be essential for improved performance; for example, there is some evidence that an anxiety reduction programme may work about as well as direct training in improving performance. In addition, researchers have established that improvements following training persist. Willis and Nesselroade (1990) reported results from a seven-year follow-up to the original Project ADEPT study. After initial training in 1979, participants received booster sessions in 1981 and 1986. Significant improvement was still evident at the long-term follow-up, even in people in their late 70s and early 80s. These results demonstrate that training effects are powerful, even in the oldest participants in Willis's research.

Piagetian research

A second major approach to the study of intelligence emphasizes the cognitive processes underlying thought rather than the product of thought. This second approach is exemplified by Piaget's theory, which focuses on the growth of knowledge and how the structure of knowledge changes over time. Because Piaget's theory is described in detail elsewhere, we shall concentrate here on its implications for adult development and ageing.

Piaget believed that formal operations marked the end of cognitive development, although there are hints that he may not have been entirely convinced of this (e.g., Piaget, 1972). In any case, researchers in this tradition have generally believed that formal operations was the culmination of cognitive development, and looked for evidence of stability in formal operational reasoning across adulthood. They found little evidence of it. Some studies report that relatively few adults demonstrate formal operational reasoning, and others show that older adults do not perform as well as younger adults on formal operational tasks.

There are several problems with this line of research, however. First, the studies were cross-sectional, opening them to criticisms based on cohort differences. Second, the age differences demonstrated may be due more to personal preference than to a lack of ability. That is, older adults may simply have a lack of interest in solving problems that demand formal logical reasoning. Third, researchers may have been looking for the wrong thing. Specifically, it is also possible that the reason for the failure to find substantial evidence for formal operational reasoning is that adults have moved on to a different type of thinking.

Postformal thought

Since the early 1970s, evidence has been mounting that adults approach certain types of problems in fundamentally different ways than adolescents. In particular, problems involving social situations, that are ill structured, or that require life experience are solved differently by middle-aged and older adults (Cavanaugh, Kramer, Sinnott, Camp, & Markley, 1985; Commons, Sinnott, Richards, & Armon, 1989). Postformal thinking involves acceptance of more than one correct solution, tolerance for ambiguity, acknowledgement of practical or real-world constraints, and acceptance of contradiction. Labouvie-Vief (1985) also argues that adult postformal thinking involves the integration of emotion with logic, and sees the main goal of adult thought as effectiveness in handling everyday life.

Wisdom

One of the relatively few positive stereotypes about ageing is that older adults become wise. Despite this belief, wisdom is seldom the focus of research on older adults' cognition. What little has been done has emphasized a connection between wisdom and expert knowledge. Smith and Baltes (1990) describe a wise person as one who has "exceptional insight into human development and life matters, exceptionally good judgement, advice, and commentary about difficult life problems" (p. 495). Wisdom is apparently not the same thing as creativity; wisdom is more related to the growth of expertise and insight whereas creativity is associated with generating a new solution to a problem. For a person to be wise, he or she needs to have accumulated relevant life-experience. In this sense, wisdom is associated with age. However, simply being old does not guarantee that one will be wise (Smith & Baltes, 1990).

PERSONALITY

Perhaps no other area in ageing research has engendered as much controversy as personality. At issue is a fundamental question: does personality change across adulthood? Answers to this question generally localize around two discrepant views. On the one hand, trait theorists believe that stability in personality is normative. In contrast, ego and cognitive theorists believe that change is the rule.

Personality traits

Many investigators have examined the relative stability of personality traits, but Costa and McCrae (e.g., 1980) are among the few who have developed a theory of personality in adulthood based on this research. In their view, personality consists of five dimensions: Factor I, Extraversion (or Surgency, including warmth, gregariousness, assertiveness, activity, excitement seeking, and positive emotions); Factor II, Agreeableness-Antagonism; Factor III, Conscientiousness-Undirectedness; Factor IV, Neuroticism (or Emotional

Stability, including anxiety, hostility, self-consciousness, depression, impulsiveness, and vulnerability), and Factor V, Openness to Experience (or Culture, or Intellect, including fantasy, aesthetics, openness to action, values, feelings, and ideas) (see also Goldberg, 1983).

Costa and McCrae's data on stability are impressive. For example, they reported correlations ranging between .68 and .85 for various traits measured 12 years apart. Other researchers report high stability over an 8-year span, while one study reported high stability over 30 years. Clearly, such evidence on very long-term stability in personality traits in individuals between 20 and 90 years of age provides strong support for the position that personality remains constant across adulthood.

Nevertheless, some researchers have found change on a few specific traits. For example, Haan, Millsap, and Hartka (1986) reported significant shifts in self-confidence, cognitive commitment, outgoingness, and warmth. However, the shifts were not orderly or universal, and did not represent a "mid-life crisis". Rather, the changes appeared to reflect life cycle experiences that forced people to change. Overall, the weight of the evidence suggests that personality traits are unlikely to change except in very specific situations.

Thomae (1980) argues that adults' personalities change only to the extent that people believe they need to change and have the motivation to carry out the process. This view fits well with notions such as personal control that also highlight the importance of people's perceptions of reality as an important determinant of behaviour. Thomae's view is also highly consistent with theories of psychotherapy that emphasize the importance of the client's desire to change as basic to the success of the therapeutic process.

Life satisfaction

As typically operationalized, life satisfaction means the degree to which people are happy with their current life situation and have positive well-being. Hundreds of studies on this issue have shown conclusively that life satisfaction is not related to age (Larson, 1978). However, life satisfaction is related to neuroticism and extraversion, as well as a host of other variables such as health, social class, gender, and immediate life situation.

Gender role identity

The shared cultural beliefs of what constitutes appropriate characteristics for women and men vary across groups. Most important for our present discussion, gender role stereotypes also vary with age. In western societies, old men are stereotypically viewed as less masculine and more peaceable, whereas old women are viewed as matriarchs overseeing extended families. Evidence from several studies indicates that changes occur in the statements adults of different ages endorse about femininity and masculinity. In general, the findings reveal a tendency for older women and men to endorse similar self-descriptions: women and men appear most different in late adolescence and young adulthood and become increasingly similar in late-middle and old age (Huyck, 1990).

Mid-life crisis

A concept central to most ego development theories of adult personality is the notion that middle-aged adults experience a mid-life crisis in which there is a general upheaval in all aspects of their lives. Despite considerable effort, researchers have largely been unable to document a crisis unique to mid-life (Haan et al., 1986). Instead, researchers report that individuals may periodically undertake a re-evaluation of their lives, but tend to do so on their own timetable rather than being driven by calendar time.

PSYCHOPATHOLOGY AND TREATMENT

There is a growing realization on the part of clinicians that assessing older adults requires a far more careful consideration of the interplay among biological, psychological, and social influences. This realization has resulted in a major emphasis on multidisciplinary assessment as a requirement for diagnosing physical and psychosocial problems. Indeed, the biopsychosocial model can be applied to all aspects of older adults' lives (Cavanaugh, 1993).

Although older adults may experience the entire spectrum of mental disorders, two dominate the literature: depression and dementia. Both represent significant problems for elderly people and in many cases present diagnostic difficulties to clinicians.

Depression

Contrary to the image that older people are prone to depression, the incidence of severe depression among elderly people is lower than that in younger adults (Nolen-Hoeksema, 1988). Older adults differ somewhat from younger adults in their symptoms of depression. Specifically, older adults may not label their sad feelings as depression, and are more likely than younger adults to show signs of apathy, subdued self-depreciation, expressionlessness, changes in arousal, withdrawal, and inadequate self-care. In addition, the physical symptoms accompanying depression (e.g., loss of appetite and sleep disturbances) must be evaluated carefully to rule out an underlying physiological problem.

Treatment of depression in elderly people is accomplished through the same types of interventions used with younger adults. Antidepressant medication (e.g., heterocyclics) are effective, but dosage levels need to be carefully monitored. Behavioural and cognitive behavioural psychotherapy are both highly effective with most older adults with depression (Gallagher & Thompson, 1983).

Dementia

The term dementia does not refer to a specific disease, but, rather, to a family of diseases that have similar symptoms. Roughly a dozen types of dementia have been identified, all of which are characterised by cognitive and behavioural deficits involving some form of permanent damage to the brain. The most common form of dementia is Alzheimer's disease.

Alzheimer's disease

Alzheimer's disease is a form of progressive, degenerative, and fatal dementia, accounting for as many as 70 per cent of all cases of dementia. Alzheimer's disease is characterized by large numbers of specific microscopic changes involving neurons: neurofibrillary tangles (abnormal, twisted fibres that are produced inside neurons), neuritic plaques (amyloid protein deposits that form in conjunction with dead neurons), and granulovacuolar bodies (deposits of granular material in the neuron). At present, definitive diagnosis of Alzheimer's disease can only be accomplished by conducting a brain autopsy. Most researchers believe that Alzheimer's disease has a genetic component, although the nature of this link remains unclear (Breitner, 1988), but mutations involving the genes responsible for the production of amyloid protein may provide an important lead (Goate et al., 1991). At present, there is no effective treatment or cure.

Alzheimer's disease is tentatively diagnosed on the basis of cognitive and behavioural changes: declines in memory, learning, attention, and judgement; disorientation in time and space; difficulties in word finding and communication; declines in personal hygiene and self-care skills; inappropriate social behaviour; and changes in personality. These symptoms tend to be vague initially and worsen steadily over time. However, the rate of deterioration is highly variable across individuals.

Caregiving

The vast majority of people with Alzheimer's disease and other forms of dementia (e.g., Huntington's chorea, multi-infarct dementia) are cared for at home by family members. Caregivers generally report feeling stressed and burdened (Kinney & Stephens, 1989). They report a host of negative effects: chronic fatigue, anger, depression, loss of friends, loss of time to themselves, dissatisfaction with other family members, physical and mental strain, lower life satisfaction, and lower well-being. Nevertheless, caregivers also show considerable ingenuity in devising strategies to help their loved ones deal with the cognitive impairments due to their disease (Cavanaugh et al., 1989).

RETIREMENT

A person's occupation has an important influence on his or her sense of identity. Withdrawing from an occupation, then, is not a trivial thing. Although it is tempting to view retirement as an all-or-none state (either one is employed or not), the actual state of affairs is far more complex. For this reason, retirement is best viewed as a complex process by which people withdraw from full-time participation in an occupation.

Deciding when to retire reflects considerations of many factors, including health, financial status, and personal attitudes toward retirement. Typically, poor health and excellent finances are the major factors in a decision to retire early. The relationship between attitudes toward retirement and the decision to retire are more complicated. In general, people who have professional occupations or who are self-employed do not look forward to retirement as much as blue-collar workers do. Middle-level managers with high incomes and good pension plans, though, are the most favourable about retiring.

Adjustment to retirement

Retirement is a stressful life transition that affects relationships with family, friends, and the community at large. Understanding how people cope with retirement is best accomplished by placing retirement in the broader context of life transitions. Thus, past behaviours and attitudes during people's employment years influence people's adjustment to retirement. For example, people who were strongly work-motivated are likely to experience more adjustment problems than people who were not. Atchley (1989) argues that successful adjustment to retirement depends on the degree to which people are able to build on their past in order to maintain a sense of continuity in their lives.

Overall, the research literature suggests that most people are satisfied with their retirement situation. One interesting trend is that retirees are increasingly concerned with financial security, and many express a desire to work at least part-time. However, the expressed desire to work appears to be based on concerns about financial security rather than a fundamental dislike for retirement. Adjustment to retirement appears to be helped by advance planning. Specifically, Kamouri and Cavanaugh (1986) reported that individuals who completed a pre-retirement education programme had more realistic views of retirement than individuals who did not participate. Holding realistic views assists individuals in understanding the lifestyle changes that occur following retirement, which in turn is an important influence on overall satisfaction.

GRANDPARENTING

Being a grandparent is an important source of identity for many older adults. How individuals act as grandparents varies considerably across individuals and cultures, ranging from playing very structured and formal roles to being remote and distant. Researchers have shown that people derive several positive meanings from grandparenthood, such as being able to indulge or spoil their grandchildren, the importance of seeing their family line continue and being perceived as a wise elder (Miller & Cavanaugh, 1990). Thomas (1986) reports that satisfaction with grandparenthood is higher in grandmothers and that the opportunity to nurture and support grandchildren is an important source of satisfaction.

Relationships between grandparents and grandchildren vary with the ages of the people involved as well as with culture. Typically, children under age 10 are closer to their grandparents than are older children and adults, and grandparents tend to enjoy younger children more. Some authors have suggested that grandmothers and granddaughters have better relationships than grandfathers and grandsons due to the importance of matrilineal kin-keeping issues in most societies.

Because of increased divorce rates in many industrialized countries, a growing issue among grandparents is contact with grandchildren after the divorce of the parents. Few places have clearly articulated policies covering grandparental visitation rights. Most grandparents desire continued contact, and see themselves as innocent victims in the parents' divorce.

WIDOWHOOD

Experiencing the death of a spouse is certainly a traumatic event for most people. Widowhood is more common for women; in western societies roughly half of women over age 65 are widows, but only about 15 per cent of the same-aged men are widowers. This difference reflects gender differences in average longevity as well as a tendency for women to marry men older than themselves.

Considerable research supports the notion that widowhood has different meanings for women and men. In general, a woman's reaction depends on the kind of relationship she had with her husband. To the extent that she defined herself in terms of her husband, widowhood causes her serious adjustment problems (Lopata, 1975). In contrast, women who define themselves in more diverse ways experience much less loss of identity following the death of their spouse.

Many people believe that the loss of a one's wife presents a more serious challenge to adjustment than the loss of one's husband. Perhaps this is because a wife is often a man's only close friend or because men may be less equipped to live out their lives alone. However, as men share more of the housekeeping tasks these gender differences begin to decrease. It is the case, however, that men are generally older when they are widowed than are women. Thus, to some extent the greater overall difficulties reported by widowers may be due to this age difference. Indeed, at least one study showed that if age is held constant, widows report higher anxiety than widowers.

Regardless of age, men have a clear advantage over women in the opportunity to form new heterosexual relationships. Interestingly, though, older widowers are actually less likely to form new, close friendships than are widows. This difference may simply be a continuation of men's lifelong tendency to have few close friendships.

ACKNOWLEDGEMENTS

The writing of this chapter was supported by NIA research grant AG09265-02 and by a research grant from the AARP Andrus Foundation.

FURTHER READING

Binstock, R. H., & George, L. K. (Eds) (1990). *Handbook of aging and the social sciences* (3rd edn). San Diego, CA: Academic Press.

Birren, J. E., & Schaie, K. W. (Eds) (1990). *Handbook of the psychology of aging* (3rd edn). New York: Van Nostrand Reinhold.

Poon, L. W., Rubin, D. C., & Wilson, B. A. (Eds) (1989). *Everyday cognition in adulthood and late life*. Cambridge: Cambridge University Press.

Sinnott, J. D., & Cavanaugh, J. C. (Eds) (1991). *Bridging paradigms: Positive development in adulthood and cognitive aging*. New York: Praeger.

REFERENCES

Atchley, R. C. (1989). A continuity theory of normal aging. *The Gerontologist, 29*, 183–190.

Baltes, P. B., & Willis, S. L. (1982). Enhancement (plasticity) of intellectual functioning: Penn State's Adult Development and Enrichment Project (ADEPT). In F. I. M. Craik & S. Trehub (Eds) *Aging and cognitive processes* (pp. 353–389). New York: Plenum.

Baylor, A. M., & Spirduso, W. W. (1988). Systemic aerobic exercise and components of reaction time in older women. *Journal of Gerontology, 43*, 121–126.

Breitner, J. C. S. (1988). Alzheimer's disease: Possible evidence for genetic causes. In M. K. Aronson (Ed.) *Understanding Alzheimer's disease* (pp. 34–49). New York: Scribner's.

Camp, C. J., & McKitrick, L. A. (1991). Memory interventions in Alzheimer's-type dementia populations: Methodological and theoretical issues. In R. L. West & J. D. Sinnott (Eds) *Everyday memory and aging: Current research and methodology* (pp. 155–172). New York: Springer-Verlag.

Cavanaugh, J. C. (1993). *Adult development and aging* (2nd edn). Pacific Grove, CA: Brooks/Cole.

Cavanaugh, J. C., Grady, J. G., & Perlmutter, M. (1983). Forgetting and use of memory aids in 20 to 70 year olds' everyday life. *International Journal of Aging and Human Development*, *17*, 113–122.

Cavanaugh, J. C., Kramer, D. A., Sinnott, J. D., Camp, C. J., & Markley, R. J. (1985). On missing links and such: Interfaces between cognitive research and everyday problem solving. *Human Development*, *28*, 146–168.

Cavanaugh, J. C., Dunn, N. J., Mowery, D., Feller, C., Niederehe, G., Frugé, E., & Volpendesta, D. (1989). Problem-solving strategies in dementia patient–caregiver dyads. *The Gerontologist*, *29*, 156–158.

Cohen, G., & Faulkner, D. (1989). The effects of aging on perceived and generated memories. In L. W. Poon, D. C. Rubin, & B. Wilson (Eds) *Everyday cognition in adulthood and late life* (pp. 222–243). New York: Cambridge University Press.

Commons, M. L., Sinnott, J. D., Richards, F. A., & Armon, C. (Eds) (1989). *Adult development: vol. 1. Comparisons and applications of adolescent and adult developmental models*. New York: Praeger.

Costa, P. T., Jr, & McCrae, R. R. (1980). Still stable after all these years: Personality as a key to some issues in adulthood and old age. In P. B. Baltes & O. G. Brim, Jr (Eds) *Life-span development and behavior* (vol. 3, pp. 65–102). New York: Academic Press.

Dixon, R. A., & Hultsch, D. F. (1983). Structure and development of metamemory in adulthood. *Journal of Gerontology*, *38*, 682–688.

Fisk, A. D., & Rogers, W. (1987) *Associative and priority learning in memory and visual search: A theoretical view of age-dependent practice effects*. Paper presented at the National Institute on Aging Conference on Aging and Attention, Washington, DC, November.

Gallagher, D., & Thompson, L. W. (1983). Depression. In P. M. Lewinsohn & L. Teri (Eds) *Clinical geropsychology* (pp. 7–37). New York: Pergamon.

Goate, A., Chartier-Harlin, M.-C., Mullan, M., Brown, J., Crawford, F., Fidani, L., Guiffra, L., Haynes, A., Irving, N., James, L., Mant, R., Newton, P., Rooke, K., Roques, P., Talbot, C., Williamson, R., Rossor, M., Owen, M., & Hardy, J. (1991). Segregation of a missense mutation in the amyloid precursor protein gene with familial Alzheimer's disease. *Nature*, *349*, 704–706.

Goldberg, L. R. (1993). The structure of phenotypic personality traits. *American Psychologist*, *48*, 26–34.

Haan, N., Millsap, R., & Hartka, E. (1986). As time goes by: Change and stability in personality over fifty years. *Psychology and Aging*, *1*, 220–232.

Hartley, A. A., & McKenzie, C. R. M. (1991). Attentional and perceptual contributions to the identification of extrafoveal stimuli: Adult age comparisons. *Journal of Gerontology: Psychological Sciences*, *46*, 202–206.

Horn, J. L. (1982). The aging of human abilities. In B. B. Wolman (Ed.) *Handbook of developmental psychology* (pp. 847–879). Englewood Cliffs, NJ: Prentice-Hall.

Howe, M. L. (1988). Measuring memory development in adulthood: A model-based approach to disentangling storage-retrieval contributions. In M. L. Howe & C. J. Brainerd (Eds) *Cognitive development in adulthood* (pp. 39–64). New York: Springer-Verlag.

Huyck, M. H. (1990). Gender differences in aging. In J. E. Birren & K. W. Schaie (Eds) *Handbook of the psychology of aging* (3rd edn, pp. 124–132). San Diego, CA: Academic Press.

Kamouri, A., & Cavanaugh, J. C. (1986). The impact of pre-retirement education programs on workers' pre-retirement socialization. *Journal of Occupational Behavior*, *7*, 245–256.

Kinney, J. M., & Stephens, M. A. P. (1989). Caregiver Hassles Scale: Assessing the daily hassles of caring for a family member with dementia. *The Gerontologist, 29*, 328–332.

Kline, D. W., & Schieber, F. (1985). Vision and aging. In J. E. Birren & K. W. Schaie (Eds) *Handbook of the psychology of aging* (2nd edn, pp. 296–331). New York: Van Nostrand Reinhold.

Labouvie-Vief, G. (1985). Intelligence and cognition. In J. E. Birren & K. W. Schaie (Eds) *Handbook of the psychology of aging* (2nd edn, pp. 500–530). New York: Van Nostrand Reinhold.

Larson, R. (1978). Thirty years of research on the subjective well-being of older Americans. *Journal of Gerontology, 33*, 109–125.

Lopata, H. Z. (1975). Widowhood: Societal factors in life-span disruptions and alternatives. In N. Datan & L. H. Ginsberg (Eds) *Life-span developmental psychology: Normative life crises* (pp. 217–234). New York: Academic Press.

McDowd, J. M., & Craik, F. I. M. (1988). Effects of aging and task difficulty on divided attention performance. *Journal of Experimental Psychology: Human Perception and Performance, 14*, 267–280.

McDowd, J. M, Filion, D. L., & Oseas-Kreger, D. M. (1991). *Inhibitory deficits in selective attention and aging.* Paper presented at the meeting of the American Psychological Society, Washington, DC, June.

Meyer, B. J. F. (1987). Reading comprehension and aging. In K. W. Schaie (Ed.) *Annual review of gerontology and geriatrics* (vol. 7, pp. 93–115). New York: Springer.

Miller, S. S., & Cavanaugh, J. C. (1990). The meaning of grandparenthood and its relationship to demographic, relationship, and social participation variables. *Journal of Gerontology: Psychological Sciences, 45*, 244–246.

Nolen-Hoeksema, S. (1988). Life-span views on depression. In P. B. Baltes & R. M. Lerner (Eds) *Life-span development and behavior* (vol. 9, pp. 203-241). Hillsdale, NJ: Lawrence Erlbaum.

Piaget, J. (1972). Intellectual evolution from adolescence to adulthood. *Human Development, 15*, 1–12.

Plude, D. J., & Doussard-Roosevelt, J. A. (1990). Aging and attention: Selectivity, capacity, and arousal. In E. A. Lovelace (Ed.) *Aging and cognition: Mental processes, self-awareness, and interventions* (pp. 97–133). Amsterdam: North-Holland.

Plude, D. J., & Hoyer, W. J. (1985). Attention and performance: Identifying and localizing age deficits. In N. Charness (Ed.) *Aging and human performance* (pp. 47–99). Chichester: Wiley.

Poon, L. W. (1985). Differences in human memory with aging: Nature, causes, and clinical implications. In J. E. Birren & K. W. Schaie (Eds) *Handbook of the psychology of aging* (2nd edn, pp. 427–462). New York: Van Nostrand Reinhold.

Poon, L. W., & Schaffer, G. (1982). *Prospective memory in young and elderly adults.* Paper presented at the annual conference of the American Psychological Association, Washington, DC, August.

Salthouse, T. A. (1984). Effects of age and skill in typing. *Journal of Experimental Psychology: General, 113*, 345–371.

Salthouse, T. A. (1985). Speed of behavior and its implications for cognition. In J. E. Birren & K. W. Schaie (Eds) *Handbook of the psychology of aging* (2nd edn, pp. 400–426). New York: Van Nostrand Reinhold.

Salthouse, T. A. (1991). *Status of working memory as a mediator of adult age differences in cognition.* Invited address presented at the American Psychological Association, San Francisco, CA, August.

Schaie, K. W., & Hertzog, C. (1983). Fourteen-year cohort-sequential studies of adult intelligence. *Developmental Psychology*, *19*, 531–543.

Smith, J., & Baltes, P. B. (1990). Wisdom-related knowledge: Age/cohort differences in responses to life-planning problems. *Developmental Psychology*, *26*, 494–505.

Thomae, H. (1980). Personality and adjustment to aging. In J. E. Birren & R. B. Sloane (Eds) *Handbook of mental health and aging* (pp. 285–301). Englewood Cliffs, NJ: Prentice-Hall.

Thomas, J. L. (1986). Gender differences in satisfaction with grandparenting. *Psychology anal Aging*, *1*, 215–219.

Willis, S. L., & Nesselroade, J. R. (1990). Long-term effects of fluid ability training in old-old age. *Developmental Psychology*, *26*, 905–910.

Yesavage, J. A. (1983). Imagery retraining and memory training in the elderly. *Gerontology*, *29*, 271–275.

velopment, the stage from about
ions, characterized by operations
erations, pre-operational period,

gos, study, the study of ageing and

in responsiveness to some stimulus or
osure.
tasis, stoppage, the maintenance of equi-
gical process by automatic compensation

p or urge on, a chemical substance secreted
gland (q.v.) and transported to another part
effect.

l design, a variable that is varied by the
r variables in order to examine its effects on the

e, to understand, the ability to think, in itself not
ted in such examples of intelligent behaviour as
and measurable by intelligence quotient (IQ) (q.v.)

n introduced by the German psychologist William
son's mental age divided by his or her chronological
omary to multiply this quotient by 100 in order to
entage of chronological age, but in contemporary psy-
es are defined statistically without reference to the ratio
age: a person's IQ is defined by reference to a hypothet-
res in a normal distribution (q.v.) with a mean (q.v.) of
ation (q.v.) of 15.
quotient.

ice (LAD) a hypothetical innately given mechanism through
acquire language, originally supposed by the linguistic theorist
be preprogrammed with certain basic rules of grammar.
permanent change in behaviour that occurs as a result of

research design in which the same sample of subjects is examined
an extended span of time, typically to investigate problems of
sychology. *Cf.* cross-sectional study.

rithmetic mean, the technical word in descriptive statistics for the
measure of central tendency, popularly known as the average. The
ite set of scores is normally calculated by adding the scores together
iding the total by the number of scores.
ental process of encoding, storage, and retrieval of information.
A) *see under* intelligence quotient (IQ).
according to DSM-IV (q.v.), a psychological or behavioural syn-
ern associated with distress (a painful symptom), disability (impair-
r more areas of functioning), and a significantly increased risk of

GLOSSARY

This glossary is confined to a selection of frequently used terms that merit explanation
or comment. Its informal definitions are intended as practical guides to meanings and
usages. The entries are arranged alphabetically, word by word, and numerals are posi-
tioned as though they were spelled out.

accommodation 1. in Piaget's theory of cognitive development, the type of adaptation in which old cognitive schemata (q.v.) are modified or new ones formed in
order to absorb information that can neither be ignored nor adapted through
assimilation (q.v.) into the existing network of 'knowledge, beliefs, and expectations. **2.** In vision, modification of the shape of the eye's lens to focus on objects
at different distances. **3.** In social psychology, the modification of behaviour in
response to social pressure or group norms, as for example in conformity (q.v.).

adolescence from the Latin *adolescere*, to grow up, the period of development
between puberty and adulthood.

adrenal glands from the Latin *ad*, to, *renes*, kidneys, a pair of endocrine glands (q.v.),
situated just above the kidneys, which secrete adrenalin (epinephrine) and
noradrenalin (norepinephrine) (qq.v.), and other hormones into the bloodstream.
See also adrenocorticotropic hormone (ACTH).

adrenalin(e) hormone secreted by the adrenal glands (q.v.), causing an increase in
blood pressure, release of sugar by the liver, and several other physiological reactions to perceived threat or danger. *See also* endocrine glands, noradrenalin(e).

adrenocorticotropic hormone (ACTH) a hormone secreted by the pituitary gland that
stimulates the adrenal gland to secrete corticosteroid hormones such as cortisol
(hydrocortisone) into the bloodstream, especially in response to stress or injury.

Alzheimer's disease named after the German physician who first identified it, a
degenerative form of presenile dementia (q.v.), usually becoming manifest between
the ages of 40 and 60, characterized by loss of memory and impairments of thought
and speech. *See also* senile dementia.

androgens from the Greek *andros*, man, *genes*, born, any of a number of male sex
hormones, notably testosterone, secreted by the testes and the adrenal glands (q.v.)
in males and in small amounts by the ovaries and the adrenal glands in females,
responsible for the development of masculine secondary sexual characteristics.

assimilation the process of absorbing new information into existing cognitive structures and modifying it as necessary to fit with existing structures. In Piaget's theory
of cognitive development, the type of adaptation in which existing cognitive schemata (q.v.) select for incorporation only those items of information that fit or can
be forced into the existing network of knowledge, beliefs, and expectations. *Cf.*
accommodation.

attachment in developmental psychology, an emotional bond between babies and their primary caretakers. In later life, any strong emotional tie or binding affection between people.

attitude a fairly stable evaluative response towards a person, object, activity, or abstract concept, comprising a cognitive component (positive or negative perceptions and beliefs), an emotional component (positive or negative feelings), and a behavioural component (positive or negative response tendencies).

authoritarian personality a personality (q.v.) type strongly disposed to racial and other forms of prejudice (q.v.), first identified in 1950, characterized by rigid adherence to conventional middle-class values, submissive, uncritical attitudes towards authority figures, aggressive, punitive attitudes towards people who violate conventional norms, avoidance of anything subjective or tender-minded, an inclination to superstition, preoccupation with strong-weak dichotomies, cynical distrust of humanity in general, a tendency towards projection of unconscious emotions and impulses, and preoccupation with the sexual activities of other people.

autonomic nervous system a subdivision of the nervous system (q.v.) that regulates (autonomously) the internal organs and glands. It is divided into the sympathetic nervous system and the parasympathetic nervous system (qq.v.).

case-study a research method involving a detailed investigation of a single individual or a single organized group, used extensively in clinical psychology and less often in other branches of psychology.

central limit theorem in statistics, a theorem showing (roughly) that the sum of any large number of unrelated variables tends to be distributed according to the normal distribution (q.v.). It explains why psychological and biological variables that are due to the additive effects of numerous independently acting causes are distributed approximately normally.

central nervous system (CNS) in human beings and other vertebrates, the brain and spinal cord.

centration Piaget's term for the tendency of children in the pre-operational period (q.v.) to focus on only one aspect of a problem at a time, one consequence of which is their failure to solve problems involving conservation (q.v.) of number, substance, mass, and volume.

choice reaction time *see under* reaction time.

chronological age *see under* intelligence quotient (IQ).

cognition from the Latin *cognoscere*, to know, attention, thinking, problem-solving, remembering, and all other mental processes that fall under the general heading of information processing.

cognitive schema (pl. schemata or schemas) an integrated network of knowledge, beliefs, and expectations relating to a particular subject; in Piaget's theory of cognitive development, the basic element of mental life.

cohort from the Latin *cohors*, company of soldiers, a group of people who share some experience or demographic trait in common, especially being of similar age (an age cohort).

concrete operations in Piaget's theory of cognitive development, a class of cognitive operations that are logical but tied to the physical (concrete) world and not abstract, and are characteristic of children between the ages of approximately 7 and 11 years, after the pre-operational period but before the stage of formal operations (q.v.) involving abstract thinking. Cf. formal operations, pre-operational period, sensori-motor period.

conformity the modification of attitudes, opinions, or behaviour in response to social pressure from group members or prevailing social norms.

formal operations in Piaget's theory of cognitive development, following the period of concrete operations at 11 years, following the period of concrete operations involving deductive reasoning. Cf. concrete operations, sensori-motor period.

gerontology from the Greek *geron*, old man, the problems associated with old age, gradual adaptation or decrease

habituation gradual adaptation or decrease class of stimuli as a result of repeated exposure

homeostasis from the Greek *homos*, same, librium in any physiological or psychological for disrupting changes.

hormone from the Greek *horman*, to stir into the bloodstream by an endocrine of the body where it exerts a specific

independent variable in experiments experimenter independently of other dependent variable (q.v.).

intelligence from the Latin *intelligere* directly observable, but manifested reasoning and problem solving, tests.

intelligence quotient (IQ) a term Stern in 1912 to denote a perscore (actual) age. It became custom express mental age as a percentage chometric practice IQ scores of mental to chronological age of IQ scores ical population of IQ scores 100 and a standard devi

IQ *see under* intelligence

dependency general disturbance disorders tests.

development over the life experience.

DSM-IV the con *Manual of Men* in 1994, replacing taining the most au

emotion from the Latin tional, short-term psycho

endocrine gland any ductless (qq.v.), that secretes hormone functions as an elaborate signal system (q.v.).

epinephrine, norepinephrine from the words for adrenalin and noradrenalin *also* endocrine gland.

factor analysis a statistical technique for a number of variables in order to reduce the dimensions, called factors, in a manner analo colours can be reduced to combinations of ju

language acquisition de which human beings Noam Chomsky to experience.

learning the relative experience.

longitudinal study repeatedly over developmental

mean short for a most common mean of a fir and then di

memory the mental a mental

death, pain, disability, or an important loss of freedom, occurring not merely as a predictable response to a disturbing life-event.

motivation the motive forces responsible for the initiation, persistence, direction, and vigour of goal-directed behaviour.

neuropsychology the study of the psychological effects of damage to the central nervous system (q.v.).

nervous system *see under* autonomic nervous system, central nervous system (CNS), parasympathetic nervous system, sympathetic nervous system.

noradrenalin a hormone (q.v.) and an important neurotransmitter in the nervous system (q.v.), also called norepinephrine, especially in United States usage.

normal distribution a symmetrical, bell-shaped probability distribution, with the most probable scores concentrated around the mean (average) and progressively less probable scores occurring further from the mean: 68.26 per cent of scores fall within one standard deviation (q.v.) on either side of the mean, 95.44 per cent fall within two standard deviations, and 99.75 fall within three standard deviations. Because of the central limit theorem (q.v.), the normal distribution approximates the observed frequency distributions of many psychological and biological variables and is widely used in inferential statistics.

oestrogen any of a number of female sex hormones.

parasympathetic nervous system one of the two major divisions of the autonomic nervous system; its general function is to conserve metabolic energy. *Cf.* sympathetic nervous system.

perception the processing of sensory information from the receptors (q.v.). *Cf.* sensation.

personality from the Latin *persona*, mask, the sum total of all the behavioural and mental characteristics that distinguish an individual from others.

pituitary gland the master endocrine gland (q.v.), attached by a stalk to the base of the brain, which secretes into the bloodstream hormones affecting bodily growth and the functioning of other endocrine glands. *See also* adrenocorticotropic hormone (ACTH).

prejudice literally pre-judgement, that is, a preconception or a premature opinion based on insufficient evidence; more specifically, a negative attitude (q.v.) towards a whole category of people, especially a minority group within society. *See also* authoritarian personality.

pre-operational period in Piaget's theory of cognitive development, the period from about 18 months to 7 years, following the sensori-motor period but before the stage of formal operations, during which object permanence is mastered and thinking is perceptually driven and intuitive rather than logical, but without mastery of conservation (q.v.). *Cf.* concrete operations, formal operations, sensori-motor period.

presenile dementia a form of dementia (q.v.) of unknown cause starting before old age. *See also* Alzheimer's disease.

product-moment correlation coefficient *see under* correlation.

progesterone a female sex hormone that prepares the uterus for the fertilized ovum and maintains pregnancy.

psychology from the Greek *psyche*, mind, *logos*, study, the study of the nature, functions, and phenomena of behaviour and mental experience.

puberty from the Latin *puber*, adult, the period of development that marks the onset of adolescence when secondary sexual characteristics emerge.

reaction time the minimum time between the presentation of a stimulus and a subject's response. In experiments involving choice reaction time, the subject is presented at unpredictable times with one of two or more stimuli, each of which requires a different response.

receptor a sense organ or structure that is sensitive to a specific form of physical energy and that transmits neural information to other parts of the nervous system (q.v.).

response any behavioural or glandular activity of a person or an animal, especially as a reaction to a stimulus (q.v.).

saccade from the French word meaning a jerk on the reins of a horse, a sudden movement of the eyes from one fixation point to another, such as occurs when reading.

schema *see* cognitive schema.

senile dementia from the Latin *senilis*, old, + dementia, dementia (q.v.) of unknown cause in old people, often associated with Alzheimer's disease (q.v.).

sensation acquisition by the body's internal and external sense organs or receptors (q.v.) of 'raw' information. *Cf.* perception.

sensori-motor period in Piaget's theory of cognitive development, the first period, before the pre-operational period, from birth until about 18 months, during which an infant functions without fully developed internal representations of objects or mental images but merely with sensori-motor schemata (q.v.). *Cf.* concrete operations, formal operations, pre-operational period.

sensory adaptation the diminution or disappearance of responsiveness that occurs when an unchanging stimulus is repeated or continued.

significance (statistical) a property of the results of an empirical investigation suggesting that they are unlikely to be due to chance factors alone. The 5 per cent level of significance has become conventional in psychology; this means that results are normally considered to be statistically significant if statistical tests show that the probability of obtaining results at least as extreme by chance alone is less than 5 per cent, usually written $p < .05$.

social skills a class of abilities to perform the forms of verbal and non-verbal behaviour required for competent social interaction in order to produce desired effects on other people.

socialization in developmental psychology, the modification from infancy of a person's behaviour to conform with the demands of society.

sociogram a pictorial representation derived from sociometry (q.v.) of the social relationships in a group.

sociometry from the Latin *socius*, a companion, and the Greek *metron*, measure, the measurement of social relationships, especially friendship patterns, within groups. *See also* sociogram.

standard deviation in descriptive statistics, a measure of dispersion or variability expressed in the same units as the scores themselves, equal to the square root of the variance (q.v.).

stereotype from the Greek *stereos*, solid, *tupos*, type, an over-simplified, biased, and above all inflexible conception of a social group. The word was originally used in the printing trade for a solid metallic plate which was difficult to alter once cast.

stimulus (pl. stimuli) any objectively discernable event capable of evoking a response (q.v.) in an organism.

subjects from the Latin *sub*, under, *jacere*, to throw, people or other organisms whose behaviour or mental experience is investigated in psychological research.

sympathetic nervous system one of the two major divisions of the autonomic nervous system; it is concerned with general activation, and it mobilizes the body's reaction to stress or perceived danger. *Cf.* parasympathetic nervous system.

testosterone one of the most important of the androgens (q.v.).

variability in statistics, the degree to which a set of scores is scattered. Thus two sets of scores with identical means (averages) may have widely different variabilities. The usual measures of variability are the variance and the standard deviation (qq.v.).

variance in descriptive statistics, a measure of the dispersion or variability (q.v.) of a set of scores; it is equal to the mean (average) of the squared deviations of the scores from their mean. *See also* standard deviation.

INDEX